THE IMPAC
COMMUNITY

CW00418240

How to Gather Evidence

Karen McArdle, Sue Briggs, Kirsty Forrester,
Ed Garrett and Catherine McKay

P

First published in Great Britain in 2020 by

Policy Press
University of Bristol
1-9 Old Park Hill
Bristol
BS2 8BB
UK
t: +44 (0)117 954 5940
pp-info@bristol.ac.uk
www.policypress.co.uk

British Library Cataloguing in Publication Data
A catalogue record for this book is available from the British Library

ISBN 978-1-4473-4394-3 paperback
ISBN 978-1-4473-4396-7 ePub
ISBN 978-1-4473-4395-0 ePdf

Cover design by Robin Hawes
Front cover image: iStock / Mordolff

Contents

List of figures and tables

Figures

Tables

Notes on the authors

Karen McArdle, FRSA, has more than 30 years' experience working in the community, primarily in Scotland and Australia. She has educated hundreds of students who work in these communities. She is an active member of the Scottish Workers' Educational Association (WEA) and the Collaborative Action Research Network, and is a trustee of the third sector organisation, Evaluation Support Scotland.

Sue Briggs has a background in community development, learning in communities, workforce development and quality management, and over many years has worked in the voluntary, private and public sectors. Capturing effectively the difference our interventions make through learning and development work in communities is an important driver for her. Having fought for many years to raise the bar of visibility for community work, Sue relishes the opportunity to contribute to this publication and to move the dialogue and focus on.

Kirsty Forrester has worked in adult learning, youth work and community development in Scotland and overseas, in public and third sector organisations, within education, health and social work departments and in both urban and rural settings. She has worked in local government in the north-east of Scotland for over ten years and is currently interested in how participatory methods can be used to increase accountability to our learners.

Ed Garrett is a community learning and development worker with Aberdeenshire Council, Scotland, as well as working for the WEA. In addition to many years' experience of the practice of community work, he also has a background in academic research and teaching. He has a particular interest in the role of community work in the generation of shared knowledge and how this links to social justice and democracy.

Catherine McKay has had over 30 years of experience in community learning and development both at local and national policy level, with a focus on adult learning, adult literacies and English for Speakers of Other Languages. She is co-editor of *Developing Communities Through Learning: Demonstrating Impact* (Nova Scientific, 2017).

Acknowledgements

We would like to acknowledge all our colleagues and students, whose community work has inspired and informed this book.

Introduction

'Every action we take impacts the lives of others around us.' (Arthur Carmazzi)

Being able to provide evidence of the value of what you do working in and with communities is clearly important for lots of good reasons that come quickly to mind. It can help secure funding and improve the long-term sustainability and profile of your work, as well as improving your own practice and keeping communities themselves informed of progress. It also can be used to meet the demands of funders, show value for money and improve effectiveness. We hope that this book is useful in these regards; it is intended to be a very practical resource for those who want to reflect on and improve how they provide evidence of what they do. The community is the focus of work for a very wide range of people – from volunteers to paid staff, in public, third and private sectors, from qualified community work professionals through to many others working in social care, health, education, planning, the arts and beyond and we all have an impact on those with whom we work.

It is important when thinking about impact to be aware that we want to show impact but the ways in which we do this themselves have an impact on our participants. This book not only concerns the methodology of generating evidence of impact, but also highlights the importance of ethical judgements about the ways in which we do this. Ethics is a theme that runs throughout this book, as the authors consider the judgements that we make about what has worked or what matters, for example, to be value judgements, which lie in the ethical domain. This is true for the judgements made by community workers but also the judgements made by the funders and decision makers who assess our evidence. Banks and colleagues (2013) refer to ethics in a practical context as 'everyday ethics', which is a term that stresses the situated nature of ethics, with a focus on qualities of character and responsibilities attaching to particular relationships, rather than ethics being a set of principles or rules.

We also think, however, that this book needs to be understood in a context that is bigger than the generation of evidence of individual projects, a context in which the dynamics of a globalised neoliberalism and a growing populism continue to justify and increase inequalities, while at the same time threatening basic democratic values. This is a context that questions the value of community work, while at the same time increasing the need for such work. In this context of both threat and need, one needs to be better at understanding the value of what is done in the community. So, as well as providing a resource for practitioners, this book is intended to be part of the process of building and communicating the value of community work at policy and strategic levels. This process is in part about building the evidence base across the sector, but also in part about building the confidence of those working with communities, to communicate the value of what they do.

The book is divided into two main parts. The first part lays out the framework that community workers need to think about when evidencing impact; the second part details the key approaches you might take when doing this process. The book does not need to be read cover to cover, as each chapter in Part II stands in its own right (although there are references made between chapters). We do, however, recommend that you read Part I before going on to look at any of the specific approaches in Part II.

Part I consists of three interlinked chapters. Chapter 1 explores the key concepts of the title of the book – community work, evidence and impact. It suggests that all community work is about transformation, whether this be of individuals or communities. Providing evidence of the impact of this transformation is integral to what one does as a community worker, and is key to the development of professional knowledge. It presents the idea of evidence as a continuum running from softer qualitative evidence to harder quantitative evidence. Impact is about building a picture of change from this continuum. Chapters 2 and 3 explore some of the complexities of this process particularly through an understanding of power. As community workers, we are negotiating power and we need to be aware of how power manifests itself in all our interactions. In this context, we need to be particularly aware of how the process of gathering evidence of impact should itself be an empowering process. Chapter 2 also looks at how knowledge is a site of power and how different ways of knowing and, therefore, types of evidence, can be valued differently. In order to manage these complexities, both political and epistemological, and be secure in our own professional knowledge, the chapter makes a strong case for the values of reflective practice and reflexivity in the production and development of our own knowledge base.

We hope that the format of the book encourages such reflective practice. At the end of each chapter there are some challenge questions, which are there for you to consider in relation to your own practice. There are also several case studies in each chapter, which are again intended as a means to enable you to reflect on what you might do; what assumptions you might have; and what you could learn from this process.

Part II starts off with what is, in some senses, the end point of the evidence-gathering process – the presentation of your findings. However, as Chapter 4 argues, you need to be thinking about how you will present your findings from the very start. The presentation of findings is the key stage in influencing what happens, in policy, professional and personal terms, after your bit of work. The chapter explores the merits of different ways of, and times for, presenting findings, and also serves as an introduction to the awareness of the self, as author of the presentation, whatever format it might take; the self informs the character of the presentation.

Chapter 5 builds further on the importance of planning in the context of evaluation. You will probably want to undertake evaluation with the evidence you gather. Evaluation is clearly closely linked to showing evidence of impact, but the two are distinct, with evaluation, a form of research, being aimed at finding out if you have been successful in what you intended to do. The chapter explores the process of evaluation planning and the need to think about how we undertake evaluation as research. Radical research is introduced as an approach that can overcome inequalities of power between researcher and researched and allow for a multiplicity of voices to lead and inform the research.

Chapters 6 to 10 outline and discuss the key methods you might use when seeking to gather evidence of impact. Chapter 6 distinguishes between different ways of observing and argues for a greater confidence in our use of observation and anecdote, as central to the community work approach. Chapters 7 and 8 cover some of the methods that people may be most familiar with – questionnaires, interviews and focus groups. Questionnaires, it is suggested, are often not used well and this is an issue both of design and context. This chapter will help you to think about both, as well as the interpretation of the data that come out of the returns. Interviews and focus groups are introduced as exciting means of gathering evidence, as they allow for the direct voice of participants. Planning and conducting interviews and focus groups are discussed with an emphasis on building an awareness of your role as interviewer or facilitator in influencing the views of the participants. Chapter 9 focuses on narrative inquiry and Chapter 10 explores collaborative and participatory approaches to gathering evidence, arguing that there are both pragmatic reasons for involving communities and participants themselves in this process – you often get better results – as well as reasons linked to the promotion of empowerment and social justice. A detailed sequencing of involving participants in a process of participatory action research is given.

Chapters 11 and 12 take a step away from the details of evidence-gathering methods and look at the broader frameworks you need to think about during this process. Chapter 11 introduces the concept of social impact as key to what we aim to do as practitioners, before exploring some of the approaches you can use to demonstrate this impact. Longitudinal studies are discussed in Chapter 12 as an important way of marshalling evidence of the long-term impacts of interventions. Given that many of the impacts of work in the community may only be fully realised in the long term, it is crucial that we have the confidence and skills to undertake such studies.

Chapters 13 and 14 explore other sources of information we can use to demonstrate evidence of impact, in addition to what we may have gathered on our own in a process known as triangulation. Chapter 13 outlines the value of management information systems (MISs) for the practitioner as well as management, while Chapter 14 looks at sources of secondary data, including that from other organisations and other research and literature. It argues that we need to ask critical questions of the relevance and ethics of such data and that it can be very useful in supporting our own evidence-gathering methods.

It is appropriate that Part II finishes with a chapter on self-evaluation. It argues that self-evaluation should provide a baseline for reflection, a process that underpins the approaches to gathering evidence explored in earlier chapters. Good self-evaluation should ensure that we continue to gather evidence of impact effectively and appropriately. As well as exploring a framework for self-evaluation, the chapter recognises some of the challenges to self that evaluation can bring in terms of personal and professional risk; being aware of the construction of our professional selves can be a good way of meeting these challenges.

The authors of this book are from a range of academic and practice backgrounds, with extensive experience of community work in the third and public sectors, as well as teaching, research and policy development. To this extent, the writing of the book has been an embodiment of some of its key themes – the importance of collaboration; the equal valuing of different sources of knowledge; and the need for the academic and the practitioner to work together in the generation of professional knowledge.

Although the book is most definitely a practical 'how to' guide to providing evidence of impact, this does not mean that it is just a practical book. In fact, it contains theory and we trust that you will find this theory not only interesting but also useful in developing your practice. Theory is essential for effective practice; it should exist with practice in a dynamic relationship, in which our understanding of each is informed by the other, in a process known as praxis. If we are only interested in theory, we may become isolated in the traditional ivory tower of academia, but if we are only interested in practice, we may not be very good at understanding and communicating our own practice. This understanding, informed by theory, is important both at the level of our own practice but also at the broader societal and international levels mentioned earlier. If, as community workers, we are serious about tackling social injustice and inequality, we need to be operating within understandings of how such issues are produced and perpetuated. Also, to promote the value of our own work, we need to understand how it can be rooted in different research traditions and theories of knowledge – rooted in these domains more than in the dominant world view with which we must often engage.

We hope that his book will assist with managing some of the challenges faced by community workers in times of increased austerity, and the need to do more with less. Showing evidence of impact can, in straitened times, not only makes us more competitive for limited funds but can enhance the quality of what we do and thereby our morale, as we generate evidence of our own effective professional practice.

References

Banks, S., Armstrong, A., Carter, K., Graham, H., Hayward, P., Henry, A., Holland, T., Holmes, C., Lee, A., McNulty, A. and Moore, N., 2013. Everyday ethics in community-based participatory research, *Contemporary Social Science*, 8(3): 263–77.

Carmazzi, A., available at quotesonleadership.net (accessed 25 March 2020).

PART I

Thinking about impact

1

Impact, evidence and transformation

Karen McArdle

Introduction: three case studies

This book aims to explain how you can implement the processes of gathering evidence of the impact of your practice in the community. We hope this book will work for you as a practical 'how to' guide, but the book also contains theoretical insights to practice and how these come together in the form of 'praxis'. The term praxis refers to the way we make meaning from experience and theory, which in turn informs our practice (Stuart et al, 2015).

This chapter explores the idea of impact with work in the community and provides an introduction to the remainder of the book, which focuses on practical ideas and examples of methods of showing this impact. The book contains case studies to show how our ideas work in the field. We hope the three case studies in this chapter are similar to work you undertake; we present them here to encourage you to start thinking about practice and hope that the questions we raise will prompt reflection about the change you make and the impact of such change. By the end of the book, you should have the answers to the questions prompted by the case studies. You may wish to try to answer these questions at the end of the individual case studies as you encounter them:

The population of Maryville is 800 and 80 people came to a meeting in the village hall to discuss the future of the village, as there were plans afoot to build another 60 houses on the edge of the village, some of which were earmarked for social housing. Using a series of questions and small group discussion, the economic, social, environmental and emotional pros and cons were discussed, led by the community worker. She helped to summarise the key point of view, which was that the houses should not be built, and helped the community to think about the best ways of communicating this to decision makers and how to gather the points of view of those who had not attended. The decision was taken by the local council to approve construction of the houses against the wishes of the community. Was this a good piece of community work and how would the community worker know?

Jean is a youth worker in Johnstown and consulted young people in the town about the choices that existed for their leisure activities. She went to a range of groups such as youth clubs and uniformed clubs, and to local schools. She also got a colleague to consult parents. She used face-to-face interviews and online survey tools to gather the information. She then presented the results to the Youth Forum, which represents young people in the town, and helped them to work out what this meant for their peers. She helped them to communicate to the local council the need for more youth clubs and youth workers in a particular suburb of the town that lacked leisure activities. A decision was taken to fund a youth worker. Was this a good piece of community work and how would the youth worker know?

Ryan works in adult learning in the voluntary sector and has run a series of reminiscence groups for elderly people who have recently been bereaved and are at risk of social isolation in the city. The groups have been funded for three years and have a membership of around ten to 12 people, mainly women. The groups, however, seem to dwindle over the course of the ten-week period for which they have been funded and at the end of this period there are usually only about five or six people left. Ryan is of the view that the groups are very important to this smaller number of people who enjoy and value the time with others and that recovering from bereavement accounts for the drop-off in attendance. Ryan is aware that the funders will want to know why there is a drop-off and that this drop-off will affect future funding for what he considers to be important groups. He decides to conduct interviews with members of one of the groups to find out and document why people are leaving and why people choose to remain. He can then feed this back to the funders. Ryan thinks this is good community work. Is he right?

The intended audience for the book

To answer the questions raised here, we begin with explaining our understandings of community work and our understandings of change, so that you can see how this book can work for you in your professional practice. We need to explain that the authors of this text are working in Scotland, where community workers are known as community learning and development workers, and the underpinning theory is educational. The authors have, however, experience between them of working internationally and in the broader fields of health; English as a Second or Other Language; planning and economic development; and social work, for example. This book, we intend, can be applied to many different discipline areas. Increasingly, government departments from a range of disciplines are adopting a community focus. For example, planning departments and housing departments in the UK are engaging in community consultations and community engagement projects to help residents to have a greater say in decisions that affect them. This book is intended for these professions too.

As we are educators by preference, we have thought about the processes that will underpin the learning in this book. We have sought to make it a largely practical text, as explained earlier. To do this, we have included case studies from a range of contexts that draw on our experience of working in the community. Reflective practice is central to the professional practice of many community workers and we have sought to ask challenge questions, as well as seek to answer them. We hope to assist you to work with ideas, with careful thought and considered judgement, and thereby to integrate learning into your own practice.

Social change or transformation

The vision that brings community workers together from many different backgrounds is the desire, we propose, for social change or transformation. A community focus is common in many different work contexts, but when we are looking for evidence of impact, it is usually change we are seeking to achieve, although we should not rule out stasis or continuity as objectives. Community work can be used for a range of purposes, but we find that the most common overarching goal for community work is to strive for the wellbeing of individuals and groups in the community and wellbeing of the community itself. The 'wellbeing' of communities is, of course, a contested concept, but here we use it to define for the individual a sense of living in hope, and for the community a shared spirit of hope. Hope is an optimistic way of thinking about the world and implies an expectation of positive outcomes.

We seek to assist you to find ways of showing the impact of what you do, to demonstrate that change has taken place to self and others. We need, of course, to explain what is meant by community work. There are terms that overlap in the field of community work and these are community engagement, community consultation, community capacity building and community development, to name just a few. When we use the generic term community work, we are referring to all of these. We would argue that community development is a process in which community engagement and community consultation are important co-processes. It is not our purpose here to provide final definitions of a field that is constantly growing and developing; rather we seek to explain and defend its complexity, as this has bearing on the work of gathering evidence of effectiveness. Whatever discipline you are working in, we would argue you are engaged in managing the challenges of complexity.

Working in the community

The challenges referred to in the previous section are the need to work in a community influenced by geography, local, national and global history. The community worker also works in a place with an idiosyncratic cultural heritage. Thinking about Scottish fishing villages in the east of Scotland, for example, we work with villages that hug a violently windswept coastline. The villages have a strong cultural heritage of being close-knit in terms of the fishing tradition and a history of being justifiably wary of external economic forces and influences that have caused a downturn in their traditional way of life through fishing quotas.

You may also need to work with population characteristics such as age, gender, sexual orientation or ethnicity. Your community may have a significant number of elderly people who run a risk of social isolation or young people in a rural community who lack a choice of many things to do. You may work with refugee populations and the relationships with the traditional inhabitants of a community. You will also need to work with common or marginalised behaviours, both negative and positive, such as drug and alcohol misuse and offending, or community volunteering and befriending. There will be local issues such as poverty, lack of transport and the need for new services such as new school buildings or community centres, for example. We also would argue that there is the community spirit or lack of it to contend with.

We are not suggesting you have to deal with all of these factors, but they will be present in some shape or form, influencing the community with which you work. Being a youth worker, for example, does not mean that the wider community does not matter. The effect of the local, national and global communities on residents needs to influence the work. The work needs to be holistic and to recognise the interrelatedness of all these factors in the life of people. This is arguably the case for all social professions, but, with community work, you are less enshrined in a system for managing populations, such as a school or hospital or care home. You need to manage a great deal of complexity and this is fundamental to community work. To gather evidence of effectiveness or change, this complexity provides pluses and minuses of advantage. The complexity suggests multiple sources of evidence on the plus side and many potential indicators of effectiveness. On the minus side there are difficulties with managing the complexity in communities and deciding on how to isolate the evidence worth gathering.

Principles underpinning community work

We seek here to define the underpinning principles of community work as they apply to a range of professions working in the community; these affect everything we do in the community, as well as being the context in which we gather evidence. Margaret Ledwith (2016) has provided useful definitions of what comprises community development. She emphasises a vision of a just and sustainable world; principles of social justice and the environment; values, which we discuss in the next chapter; the process of critical consciousness; collective action; theories of power, disempowerment and empowerment; and context that is practice-situated in political times. The authors of this book have discussed their own understanding of the principles that underpin community work and in our definition they are linked to process, values, context and a vision for change.

The key principles that underpin community work, in our opinion, are:

- a commitment to facilitating change in the community;
- a concern for all members of a community or a community population;
- a commitment to community empowerment, participation and democracy;
- a commitment to equality of opportunity;
- an awareness of the intersubjectivity/interrelatedness of community influences.

Change is central to community work and the commitment to facilitating change is also central to our understanding of community work. This involves having a vision of what one is seeking to achieve when working with individuals and groups. We share Margaret Ledwith's commitment to social justice, that it is 'possible to create a world in which everyone and everything is encouraged to flourish, a democracy based on participation and collective wellbeing' (2016, p 6).

Our second principle relates to inclusion and avoidance of marginalising, or not working with, marginalised groups. It is about valuing everyone and being concerned for the wellbeing of everyone in a community. This links to the commitment to community empowerment, participation and democracy, which are key principles relating to power and the need to be aware of this in all our work. Equality of opportunity is a value that we believe is essential to community work, not least because bias must be avoided for trust and respect to be present in work in the community. Finally, an awareness of the interrelatedness of community influences is crucial to the processes we implement. It is not a uni-dimensional field of work. We cannot think about community without thinking about history, geography and culture, and managing its complexity in ways that allow us not to be overwhelmed by the multiplicity of influences but that synthesise the complexity into manageable priorities.

There can now be no doubt that engaging with communities is central to effective work in a range of professions. Engaging communities in health, for example, is central to promoting health and reducing health inequalities. Policy makers are seeking more and more to involve people increasingly in health service planning. Community involvement in the design, governance and delivery of services can improve health and make policy more sustainable (Wallerstein, 2006). Wellbeing at community level is facilitated through this work, with gains in social capital, social cohesion and fostering partnership working (Milton et al, 2011).

Statistics and Stories

Gathering evidence that change has occurred is a very important dimension of the work of community workers. 'Statistics and

Stories' was the name of an action research project undertaken in Scotland in 2015 funded by the government agency, Education Scotland. This project asked community workers exactly why they felt gathering evidence of impact was important. They came up with a range of answers that fell broadly in the fields of:

- decision making by politicians and funders;
- personal and professional development of the community worker;
- knowledge of the work and how to improve it.

Knowing if something has worked, how it has worked, and to what extent it was considered to be important by respondents in the research project was important to the community worker, so he or she so could maintain, adapt or discontinue a particular professional activity. It was also considered to be important for knowing what further skills might be needed for the project or for the individual worker. Influencing the decision making of others, in particular funders, was considered to be appropriate as a driver for gathering evidence, as increasingly funders wish to see evidence of impact in both proposals and reports of projects. In the public sector, gathering evidence was considered to be important to influencing policy, which may secure further funding or rolling out of a project to other areas, as well as ensuring that policy is influenced by good practice.

Personal knowledge of the effectiveness of what is done contributes to confidence, self-esteem and the quality of work-life for the community worker. In addition, it provides an opportunity to provide feedback and celebrate outcomes for participants or residents. Accordingly, reasons for gathering evidence cannot be separated from the stakeholders in any project. These stakeholders include funders, policy makers, professionals and participants.

To summarise, gathering evidence is important for the supervision and management of staff; for enabling the practitioner to respond to the findings; and for stimulating reflection on practice. Evidence gathering will also help to establish whether an intervention is contributing to the aims of the organisation; whether it is meeting its own objectives or outcomes; and whether it is working as intended and what changes, if any, should be made to practice. Finally, it enables us to celebrate at all levels the success of a change and to prove it works and can be extended or rolled out elsewhere.

Statistics are often a source of discomfort for those working in the social or 'people' professions, but are important as evidence. Alone they can be bland, sterile and uninformative, but coupled with stories that show the quality of an intervention they can be illuminating, concrete and exact. In our research on statistics and stories, we found that community workers considered a blend of these two factors to be strongest and most convincing.

> An important piece of work in Scotland when inspected showed the effectiveness of establishing a football team for young people who were considered to be a nuisance and causing trouble. The football team was considered to be a great hit by the young men involved, who were able to tell stories of moving away from troubled and challenging behaviour. Statistics from the local police force showed a decrease in offending behaviour among young people over a relatively short timescale. Statistics and stories came together in this piece of collaborative gathering of evidence.

Governments are increasingly keen to evaluate the effectiveness of community development programmes and much of the language of their output approaches is not relevant to projects where process and participation are the emphases (Craig, 2003).

Defining change and impact

Seeking change is something that is common to the social professions in a community context. Change may seek to empower local people, or assist a community with a transition to a new state of affairs. Empowerment and transition therefore have a lot to do with change. Other words from a thesaurus that provide a wide perspective on change and its complex character are adjustment and advance, both of which have positive connotations. Change may be thought of as making a difference or contributing to innovation or modification of the existing state. Transformation is also a positive dimension of change and we shall discuss this further later in this chapter. Reconstruction and diversification can also be products of change. Craig (2003) suggests that ideas about change should have three attributes:

- Plausibility – does evidence and common sense suggest that the activities will lead to desired outcomes?
- Doability – will resources be available to make the desired change?
- Testability – is the change susceptible to credible evaluation?

So, when we are thinking about change, it is in our interests to consider the quality of change we are seeking. Is it modification or revolution? Is it a process like transition or an endpoint such as making a difference?

While change is generally a positive term in a community work context, the dictionary definitions of impact are more negative, implying shock, collision, breakage and bouncing. It is arguably a term used in the social professions to underscore the sheer power of what is or can be done. It has become a little softer in meaning over time and is commonly used to mean 'making a difference' or 'having an effect on' something. A more negative interpretation of the use of the term impact is that it has become essential because the professions find it difficult to show the effect of what they do and accordingly need to emphasise the power of what is done to funders, policy makers and decision makers through the use of language that asserts the strength of what is done. Furthermore, neoliberals might argue that anything less than a strong impact is not worth funding or supporting.

The relationship between impact and change is that the quality of the change that occurs is defined by the quality or quantity of the impact that has taken place. Change may be either positive or negative, desired or undesired, and impact helps to define the character of the change that has taken place. Our projects undoubtedly achieve change to some extent, but the impact helps us define the quality and extent of the change.

Lichfield (1996), in a book about community impact evaluation in the planning profession, describes impact in more neutral and simple terms, as the effect of a specific cause. He also describes it as a change in an environmental context over a specified period – a change that would not have occurred if an activity had not been initiated. This summary of his definitions, which are in fact quite technical in the original, is helpful. He further describes two dimensions of impact: direct impact, which results from the project input, and indirect impact, which is generated as a side effect of the project. Impact may be cumulative, he explains, short, medium and long term; permanent and temporary; reversible, irreversible, irretrievable. Impact can be positive and beneficial, negative and harmful.

We are concerned in this book with exploring the scale, quality and significance of impact. Scale refers to the size of the impact. Did our work affect one person or a whole community of 30,500 people, for example? The quality of impact refers to the nature and also the strength of the impact. Did our work affect people in a particular way, such as generating enhanced community spirit, and was this widespread? Finally, significance is important. This is more difficult to pin down and refers to why it matters. So our impact on community spirit matters for reasons linked to society caring that people have a sense of wellbeing in their communities; it matters because it costs less in terms of services for unhappy people; it matters because community spirit may lead to additional volunteering; and there are sure to be other significances. You may have spotted the link to values and judgements that are inherent in scale, quality and significance. Scale is not always a numerical judgement. The term widespread can mean, for example, 100 or 1,000 people. Scale can mean having a 'large' impact, where the term 'large' needs to be defined further. Similarly, quality and significance are qualitative terms and are linked to the value placed on ideas and the services described. This valuing and its significance to impact are discussed further in Chapter 2.

There are a number of dimensions along which we might seek to gather evidence. These are summarised well by Stuart and colleagues (2015), who describe the difference between outcome and process evaluation. Outcome evaluation considers whether established targets have been met and whether the effects achieved were those that were intended. Process evaluation looks at what is going on in an intervention, such as why a drama club is good at reducing youth nuisance. Distance travelled is a different dimension as it seeks to understand ground gained in an intervention. It may involve looking at situations before and after an intervention or it may simply explore the quality of the journey of an individual in a programme. Impact evaluation has the purpose of exploring exactly what is different or has changed. Impacts, it must be emphasised, are not always intended or short term in character. Impact may be forecast in the future; as community work is often long term in character.

> 'If it hadn't been for you, I don't know where I would have been when I was in my teens. I was heading for disaster and had no idea what I wanted to do with my life. I would have got pregnant at the earliest chance as I had no idea of any other way to live and it would mean someone would love me.'

The quotation is from a woman, Julia, in her forties with whom Karen McArdle had worked many years before in Australia. They met after a very long separation of lives and Julia told Karen that she had been heading towards a teenage pregnancy because she felt unloved. Karen, through youth work, had helped her to find alternatives through work on self-esteem and confidence building. The effect of the work was apparent to this participant in the long term if not the short term

This is not a book solely about evaluation, although evaluation approaches are central to the processes described in this book. Evaluation, we suggest, is to judge the value of something in a thoughtful way, but the term has, however, become associated over time with research processes and methodologies. Most textbooks about evaluation will take you through a slightly modified research process. This book is a text about convincing self and others about the impact of what we do, which is linked to evaluation but may or may not involve research processes or involvement of all stakeholders; the latter is a necessary feature of formal evaluation. Often evaluation has the external viewer as its audience. We are seeking evidence to show the effectiveness of what we do. This evidence may well embrace research data, but it can take other forms too, as will become clear later in this book when we discuss the methods you can use to gather evidence.

Transformation

As the authors share an educational interest and background, they seek actively in their work evidence of transformation of the individual and the community. Transformation is moving from one state to another, a process transacted through personal or community experience. We have adopted the model of learning of Peter Jarvis, as this is the model of learning that, we propose, is most relevant to the lives of adults. Jarvis (2006) proposes that learning always begins with an experience, an event in unknown circumstances for which people are unprepared or do not know exactly how to respond to. The essence of learning is that the initial feeling of confusion or absence transforms into knowledge, competence, attitude, values and emotions. In the course of learning, the individual integrates the transformed contents of the initial disorientating situation into his/her own life history and a new person is 'formed', one who possesses more experience. The word transformation has a quality to it of significant change and difference. We propose it applies to communities in the same way that it applies to individuals, embracing the notion of change in form to a new and positive identity.

We view the concept of evidence as forming a continuum, where at the one extreme evidence may be anecdotal and relatively informal, as shown in Figure 1.1. At the other extreme, evidence may be strong and robust, and comprise formal research data. Both extremes are valuable, as anecdotal/informal evidence, often dismissed as invalid or useless, can be used cumulatively and to bolster other forms of evidence. Strong and robust data are clearly useful, but this type of evidence can have a negative side as it takes a long time to generate and is not always accessible in its presentation to its potential audience. Most evidence, we suggest, is located somewhere between the two extremes.

Anecdotal evidence may be defined as being largely descriptive. It is a narration of the experience of a phenomenon

Figure 1.1: The evidence continuum

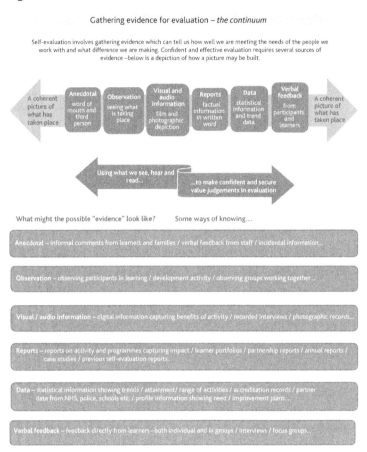

Gathering evidence for evaluation – *the continuum*

Self-evaluation involves gathering evidence which can tell us how well we are meeting the needs of the people we work with and what difference we are making. Confident and effective evaluation requires several sources of evidence –below is a depiction of how a picture may be built.

What might the possible "evidence" look like?   Some ways of knowing....

Anecdotal – informal comments from learners and families / verbal feedback from staff / incidental information...

Observation – observing participants in learning / development activity / observing groups working together...

Visual / audio information – digital information capturing benefits of activity / recorded interviews / photographic records...

Reports – reports on activity and programmes capturing impact / learner portfolios / partnership reports / annual reports / case studies / previous self-evaluation reports...

Data – statistical information showing trends / attainment/ range of activities / accreditation records / partner data from NHS, police, schools etc. / profile information showing need / improvement plans...

Verbal feedback – feedback directly from learners –both individual and in groups / interviews / focus groups...

in community work. It is a story about how things are. It may be a case study. It is sometimes based on hearsay, but we argue that it can be very convincing if used appropriately, as the following example from my own practice shows.

> Angeline came to the community centre for the first time in a state of distress. She said she was worried about schoolwork and at first would not open up about the problem. After an hour's discussion about her schoolwork, I noticed she had bruises on her arms and asked her where they came from. It took another

while before she began to talk about her boyfriend, Dean, and how he could get angry at the slightest thing. We discussed relationships and what to expect from them and Angeline explained that schoolwork was fine really, but her relationship with Dean was affecting her concentration at school. I suggested a course on relationships and sexuality that she could attend. I later heard that she had gone on the course and had finished with Dean, and that the teachers were pleased that her schoolwork was improving.

Angeline's story is anecdotal and based on hearsay, but, if coupled with stories of other young people in similar circumstances, it can be evidence of good practice. It would not work well on its own, as we do not know the causes of the break with Dean and whether the community worker's suggestion of the course had been helpful to Angeline, but an accumulation of anecdotal evidence can be convincing. We could, of course, have asked Angeline about her experiences to strengthen the anecdotal evidence.

Strong and robust evidence is not necessarily in the form of research. We have used the term 'robust' to describe evidence as dictionary definitions point to sturdiness and fullness, like freshly ground coffee, whereas the term 'rigorous' can be considered harsh and grim. It is not as accessible as robustness, as rigour commonly refers to quantitative statistical studies. We consider that strong and robust evidence often, but not always, uses a statistics and stories approach, blending quantitative evidence or data with anecdote, stories and qualitative data. To use the research term, triangulation is important. Thinking of Cubism in the arts, Picasso would get close to the 'quintessential truth' of a chair by painting it from above, below and the side all on one canvas. Making an evidential argument involves, as Picasso might do, bringing to bear on the topic a range of different perspectives, and each does not necessarily need to stand on its own.

Fraser was a community worker and worked with a club of unemployed 16–24-year-olds in Wales, helping them learn how to apply for jobs. He told his supervisor the following story.

'Yeah, it's been great. I've had a brilliant attendance every week and they've all had a fantastic time. They've developed in confidence and some have got jobs, so it's been successful. We've had a few complaints about the noise but it's only because we run at the same time as the bridge club in the community centre and they just don't understand that youngsters need their music loud. I've tried to tell them to turn it down and I've tried explaining to the bridge club but nothing works.'

This is not strong or robust evidence; it is not even anecdote, as it is a rant about the work. Fraser would be more convincing if he explained the number of people who attended and how often. How he knew they were having a fantastic time would be helpful and what they thought of the educational programme and what they had learnt. It would be useful to know how many people had got jobs and whether they ascribed this to the programme he had been running. The noise issue is incidental and could be resolved with a timetable change, negotiated rules for the young people about noise, or perhaps a change to the venue. We shall discuss later in this book the importance of building evidence gathering into the plans and implementation of projects of this kind.

The number and quality of the sources of evidence obviously matter. A professional opinion on a subject is valuable, as is direct experience of a service. So, at the anecdotal end of the continuum, it is too easy to reject one's own professional judgement, which may be based on careful observation and many years' experience, or on a thoughtful judgement of the behaviour of others. It may need to be justified, but it can form evidence. Direct experience of a service may be anecdotal but is very valuable. Participants themselves are a sound and convincing source of evidence, as they know a service or intervention at the cutting edge.

At the other end of the continuum, there is great credibility surrounding work done that involves research data generated by an external evaluator. There are many pros and cons of this type of evaluation. The evaluator has arguably no axe to grind and can take a more objective viewpoint. This needs to be balanced against a lack of direct involvement in the nitty-gritty of a project, for example, or a lack of knowledge of the fear or disquiet they may inspire in vulnerable participants, for example, in involving them in a research process with a stranger.

The bigger picture

The practice of gathering evidence around individual projects is clearly valuable and important for a multiplicity of reasons, especially influencing external funders and internal supervisors, as well as contributing to the quality of practice in many dimensions. We hope this will become increasingly clear in the course of this book. We are conscious, however, that sometimes this feels like 'tinkering around the edges' (McArdle et al, 2017) of what are complex and multifaceted issues, often linked to poverty and social injustice. We contend that while the individual can manage the individual project, these projects need to come together into a swell of evidence that contributes to more radical social change. We contend that there is a need (derived from McArdle et al, 2017) for the following:

- *Clearer understanding of how community work activates change, with clear, concise, comprehensive, well-written case studies portraying a wide range of contexts.* We think there is insufficient writing about case studies of community work that achieve change. We need to build a bulwark of successful case studies to raise awareness of the effectiveness of community work, work that can be expensive and time-consuming. It is often difficult to communicate the impact of what we do, and this is discussed further in Chapter 10, but we need to show how community work is an effective solution to many social challenges to ensure this effective method continues to be funded.
- *Longitudinal case studies, as the change we seek cannot be achieved overnight.* Often the impact we seek to make is long term and it is important to be able to show that waiting for impact can be important. The challenges of social justice and poverty,

for example, have a long history, and attitudinal change can be slow. We should embrace longitudinal vision and the longitudinal methods of showing the impact of what we do.

- *Greater commitment by practitioners to showing evidence of success.* Harland and Morgan (2006) found that the majority of their youth work respondents felt that youth work could not and should not be measured, and Smith (2003) argues that organising youth work around concepts like outcomes, targets, curriculum and issues means there is a danger of losing the relationship as a defining feature of youth work practice. We agree that relationship is important, but we are of the view that practitioners need to develop more of a commitment to gathering evidence of effectiveness for the justification of their work and to improve their services to participants.

- *Higher education establishments that educate the workers of tomorrow to have a greater commitment to these processes.* We are aware that higher education institutions often teach research methods but do not seek to develop the broader commitment to gathering evidence of effectiveness. It is crucial for future practitioners to understand how to do this evidence gathering, and research contributes to this, but a focus on maintaining the future of the community profession through many kinds of evidence is important in times of austerity and budget cuts.

- *Insistence by funders that outcomes are appropriate for needs in communities and measures of success are achievable and are able to be supported by clear evidence.* We are aware of circumstances where funders require us to meet unachievable or unconvincing or unneeded outcomes. This places considerable strain on practitioners and is not good for the goals of transformation that we suggest community work can meet. We hope this book will be read by funders and others with a financial interest in impact, so that they can learn that needed and achievable goals are the ones to be funded.

- *A stronger policy influence for this kind of work.* Who is lobbying? Who is listening? Are they armed with the best examples of success? Policy is a strong influence on funders and implementers. We consider that policy could be stronger in the community dimension of work and we also consider that practitioners should be lobbying policy makers and should have a resource to back their arguments of good examples of practice, founded on evidence of good practice.

- *A shift from predominantly local interventions, important as they are, to more global approaches aiming for change on a big scale.* We suggested earlier that we may run the risk of tinkering at the edges of social change, and we believe it is crucial that those who gather evidence of effectiveness should come together to develop approaches for change that are more national and international than local. There are a number of representative organisations that can assist with this aim and we would encourage them to play a role in this regard.

There is a role for you to place yourself in this bigger picture and to consider how, beyond your immediate work, you can contribute to the bigger picture of poverty and social injustice to work towards the wellbeing of communities. We hope this book will assist you at local level to gather evidence of your effectiveness, but we would urge you to use this evidence in a larger frame to make social change a broader movement.

Chapter 2 focuses on the important dimension of values and links to power and empowerment in gathering evidence, before the book moves on to Chapter 3, describing the ways in which this can be done. We have begun to discuss impact and change in this chapter at the local level and in the context of the bigger picture. Many of the words we have used so far imply judgement such as quality, quantity, evaluation and character of change, for example, and we need to be clear about what is 'right' in terms of what we do in gathering evidence; it involves honest, careful and sensitive judgement.

Challenge questions

1. What changes do you want to make in your practice?
2. How could you contribute to the bigger picture?

References

Banks, S., Armstrong, A., Carter, K., Graham, H., Hayward, P., Henry, A., Holland, T., Holmes, C., Lee, A., McNulty, A., Moore, N., Nayling, N., Stokoe, A. and Strachan, A. (2013) Everyday ethics in community-based participatory research, *Contemporary Social Science*, 8(3): 263–77.

Briggs, S. (2015) *The Evidence Continuum: Training Notes*, Aberdeen: Aberdeenshire Council.

Craig, G. (2003) *Towards the Measurement of Empowerment: The Evaluation of Community Development*, Hull: University of Hull.

Harland, K. and Morgan, A. (2006) Youth work in Northern Ireland: an exploration of emerging themes and challenges, *Youth Studies Ireland*, 1(1): 4–18.

Jarvis, P. (2006) *Towards a Comprehensive Theory of Human Learning: Theory and Practice*, London: Routledge.

Ledwith, M. (2016) *Community Development in Action: Putting Freire into Practice*, Bristol: Policy Press.

Lichfield, N. (1996) *Community Impact Evaluation*, London: UCL Press.

McArdle, K., Briggs, S., Forrester, K., Harper, C. and Mackay, C. (2017) *Developing Learning in Our Communities: Evidence of Impact*, Hauppauge, NY: Nova Scientific.

Milton, B., Attree, P., French, B., Povall, S., Whitehead, M., Popay, J. (2011) The impact of community engagement on health and social outcomes: a systematic review, *Community Development Journal,* advance access 23 June 2011.

Smith, M. (2003) From youth work to youth development, *Youth and Policy*, 79: 46–59.

Stuart, K., Maynard, L. and Rouncefield, C. (2015) *Evaluation Practice for Projects with Young People: A Guide to Creative Research*, London: Sage.

Wallerstein, N. (2006) *What is the Evidence on Effectiveness of Empowerment to Improve Health*, Copenhagen: WHO Regional Office for Europe, 37.

2

Power, empowerment, impact and voice

Karen McArdle

Introduction

In this chapter, we discuss the importance of values and the link to power and empowerment that is a purpose central to work in the community in democratic countries. We discuss voice, which is making the perspectives of the people with whom we work heard by ourselves and by others. We also introduce ethical choices, which must be applied to our activities linked to gathering evidence. We return to ethics frequently in this text, as we think ethics are fundamental to the processes of gathering evidence because they govern how it 'should' be done and the 'right' way of doing these processes.

What is right in terms of what we do in community work and in gathering evidence is linked to morality and the following questions:

- Why we do what we do?
- How we do what we do?
- How does this link to ideas about self and others?

Morals, as Driver (2007) explains, comprise those things one 'ought' to do. Moral norms, with which this book is concerned, primarily, as Driver explains, concern our interactions with others in ways that have significance to the latter's wellbeing. If we do something that could harm or benefit others, Driver explains, this is arguably a moral matter.

There are many examples of ways in which things have been done that are linked to what most people consider to be atrocities. We can perhaps all agree that genocide is not acceptable, but many of our choices of what to do in community work are less clear-cut. Beneficence is a useful term – it means we do what is in the best interests of humanity – but we then have to struggle with the question of who decides what is best. In community work, we often make judgements about what is in the best interests of a community, which puts us in a very powerful position. It is important to work in the community that we are clear about why we do what we do and how we choose to do it, as it affects others and those effects can be good or bad.

Self-knowledge is important in community work so we can be clear about what we do and why. Reflexivity is also important; it may be linked to reflection and critical reflection. Reflexivity is the process of a continual internal dialogue and critical self-evaluation of the practitioner's positionality, and active acknowledgement and explicit recognition that he/she may affect the outcomes of generation of data or evidence (Berger, 2013). At its simplest, we need to be aware that gender, race and sexual orientation of the practitioner, for example, may influence the evidence we generate.

Values and virtues

Going back to morality, this is a term that embraces ethics, values and good old-fashioned virtues. Each of these is important to what we do to generate evidence. Values, or deeply held beliefs, that commonly underpin work in the community, are those of equality, inclusion and, more recently, social justice. For us, the authors of this book, as educators, the importance of lifelong learning is a key belief or value that we share. We suggest that values have become a little bland through overuse over time. We can all claim that we hold these values, but do they manifest themselves in our work? They are not easy to realise in practice. We still contend, however, that equality and inclusion are important in democratic societies. Social justice is not a value that is universally held to be important in many democracies, where some people and political parties believe that you get what you work for yourself. We, however, think social justice to be important to the wellbeing not just of the individual but also of the community. We refer frequently to wellbeing and we need to be clear what this means. We adopt the definition of Jenny Spratt, as living a life of value, the value being determined by the individual. This value will be different for every person.

We believe that old-fashioned virtues, which may be considered to be values in action (McArdle et al, 2013), are an important way of thinking about the deep-seated values we hold. Pring (2004) distinguishes between moral virtues and intellectual virtues in discussing research. Moral virtues include, he suggests, courage, perseverance, honesty, caring for others, welfare and concern for others. Intellectual virtues refer to truthfulness, openness of mind, concern for accuracy, interest in clarity of communication and impartiality. We consider all of these virtues to be important in the processes of gathering evidence.

> By virtue I mean the disposition, deep and enduring, which motivates a person to pursue a course of action, despite difficulties and challenges, which the person conceived to be good and appropriate. Any list of virtues, therefore, embodies the values which prevail in a social or cultural tradition. (Pring, 2004, p 184)

If we ask practitioners what makes a good community worker, we usually get the following kinds of answers: honesty; commitment; resilience; respect; good humour; perseverance; patience; tolerance; trust. These are all virtues. Virtues are values in action and are what we hope you will bring to bear on the processes associated with community work, in general, and gathering evidence of change in particular. You might like to jot down your own answer to the question of what makes a good community worker.

Ethics

Ethics are also linked to morality and it is important, in thinking about the rights of the people with whom you work, that your evidence-gathering processes are virtue-driven. Ethics, also known as moral philosophy, is a branch of philosophy that involves systematising, defending and recommending concepts of right and wrong. Ethics studies moral behaviour and how one should act. Typically, the word ethics refers to something formal such as ethical guidelines, whereas morality refers to everyday conduct (Brinkmann and Kvale, 2015).

Ethics are rules of conduct that people adopt when they act in social contexts. Ethical behaviour is underpinned by systems of universal moral values that are characteristic of a particular social group, society or culture (Ransome, 2013). Accordingly, the people who gather evidence, research and evaluate have a system of underpinning moral values. Ethics seeks to resolve questions dealing with human morality – concepts such as good and evil and how we should behave. Moral philosophy considers how human lives should be lived and so is terribly important to our work in the community.

> Lydia is interested in how her work with girls on their relationships together and ways of avoiding internet/ social bullying has worked. She decides to observe current interaction between the girls at the youth club to gain evidence of the effectiveness of the programme, as she had previously seen bullying behaviour. She know that, if she tells them she is doing this, she will make them behave differently, so she is just going to watch in secret and write her findings up later.

It may be argued that Lydia is deceiving the girls. She reported after the event that, while it was an interesting exercise, she felt uncomfortable doing it.

Ethics are usually linked to four principles, of which avoiding deception is one, and feeling uncomfortable is often a trigger to help us think about the ethics of what we are doing. These principles are:

- avoiding harm;
- avoiding deception;
- maintaining anonymity and confidentiality;
- ensuring there is informed consent.

Avoiding harm seems relatively straightforward. It can, however, be difficult, as we cannot always, if ever, predict people's reactions to what we do. A colleague, for example, was interviewing a friend about her choice to work as a teacher. This brought up memories of parental expectations that were negative, and the teacher burst into tears. The colleague immediately stopped the discussion and changed from interview to friendship role, which was an appropriate and ethical thing to do.

Avoiding deception is important, but we know of community workers being concerned about tackling social isolation through befriending, offering free coffee and biscuits to encourage people to attend a centre where befriending can take place. The befriending dynamic is not mentioned, as it might put people off. This is deception, but is it justifiable? An ethical judgement says probably not, but we often need to make ethical choices.

In another example, staff members in the planning department of a local government authority wanted to consult the local community about a new school that would have community facilities. The decision had already been taken about where the community block of rooms would be located, but the staff wanted to appear open to the community and needed feedback on the rest of the building, so they asked the community to comment on how many community rooms there should be and where they should be located. They in effect pretended that the decision had not been made. This was unethical and dishonest.

Confidentiality, if promised, should be unbreakable, but we have heard it broken many a time in the coffee room: "You should have heard what Jimmy said. It was unbelievable!" This kind of thing is highly unethical and should not be condoned. Similarly, we should be careful about identifying people in reports or presentations unless they agree to it. It is important to use pseudonyms and hide identifying details where necessary.

Informed consent is crucial and must be freely given. Providing full details of what you are doing and why is also crucial and should be done in a way that is accessible to the community with which you are working. Informed consent means that people can choose to leave the process at any time, and consent often needs to be renegotiated by checking at suitable junctures that the participant is still happy to continue.

As ethics are such an important aspect of community work, Box 2.1 provides some suggestions for further reading.

Box 2.1 Further reading on ethics

BERA (British Educational Research Association) (2011) *Ethical Guidelines for Educational Research*, London: BERA.

Driver, J. (2007) *Ethics: The Fundamentals*, Oxford: Blackwell.

Ransome, P. (2013) *Ethics & Values in Social Research*, Basingstoke: Palgrave Macmillan.

Vardy, C. and Vardy, P. (2012) *Ethics Matters*, London: SCM Press.

Rights

These ethical principles are useful, but are by no means sufficient in thinking about ethics. We must also think about rights. People in democracies have rights, we suggest, that are not limited to the right to vote and to legal rights, but include the right to be treated with honesty and respect. Honesty is again not always clear-cut, but our gathering of evidence needs to be done honestly, telling people clearly and exactly what we are doing. Similarly, working by stealth in community work – that is, failing to reveal to community members the true intentions of the work – is dishonest but widely undertaken. This disrespects the ability of participants to make choices, sensible choices, about whether to be involved.

Treating people with respect is part of practising values of equality. To disrespect someone is to use a power relationship badly. Foucault (1990) argues that power is everywhere and informs everything we do, shaping society and transactions and the way we think about the world. We agree with this perspective. In the next section, we discuss a fundamental principle that underpins community work – community empowerment.

Power and empowerment

Commonly, community work is stimulated by a desire to empower individuals or the community itself. There are different definitions of 'empowerment', but they typically fall into two types: those that see empowerment as an outcome and those that see it as a process. We choose a definition that embraces both. Community empowerment is a process that involves continual shifts in power relations between different individuals and social groups in society. It is also an outcome and may be, for example, a product of the redistribution of resources and decision-making authority (power over) or the achievement of an increased sense of self-determination and self-esteem (power from within) (Laverack, 2006). The complexity of the context for seeking empowerment is illustrated in the health field, where there is an association between increased morbidity and mortality, and social, structural and physical factors in the environment, such as inadequate housing, poor sanitation, unemployment, exposure to toxic chemicals, occupational stress, minority status, powerlessness or alienation, and the lack of supportive interpersonal relationships (Israel et al, 1994).

We also need to think about what is a community, in the empowerment context. We probably all know the definitions of geography, ethnicity and neighbourhood but Israel and colleagues (1994) suggest it is characterised by the following elements:

- membership – a sense of identity and belonging;
- common symbol systems – similar language, rituals and ceremonies;
- shared values and norms;
- mutual influence – where community members have influence and are influenced;
- shared needs and a commitment to meeting them;
- shared emotional connection – where members share common history, experiences and mutual support.

If we are seeking community empowerment, it is likely that, if these elements do not exist, we shall be working to seek to ameliorate this. We may also be seeking individual empowerment, which includes the ability of people to gain understanding and control over personal, social, economic and political forces, in order to take action to improve their lives. Empowerment at the individual and community levels is closely interrelated. The empowered community also has the ability to influence decisions in wider systems and structures, so empowerment is closely linked to democracy.

If we accept, as many people do, Foucault's (1990) description of power as being in every part of society and being implicit in discourse and language, we acknowledge that we cannot empower people in all facets of their lives. They need to empower themselves, but we can help. Power is very subtle and complex, and informs all our social interactions. When we go to a council office as a customer or to the doctor's surgery as a patient, or go to see a social worker, there are social and cultural power issues affecting us. They have some control over our wellbeing. The people we meet may choose to use their authority in ways that belittle us or they may treat us as equals; they may choose to be aware of, and minimise, the power imbalance. Similarly, when we gather evidence, we use people to generate information and we must be aware of the power we have to manipulate people and information in this role. Some argue that empowering others is impossible, but we can influence others and educate others to understand ways in which they can take control of negative situations in which they find themselves.

The multidimensional and multilevel character of community empowerment means it is a complex process. Empowerment is not just an individual psychological construct; it is organisational, political, sociological, economic and spiritual. The organisations in which we work may or may not be empowering, and we need to work with both individuals and groups to facilitate empowerment. The community itself must be willing to participate and this relies on the process meeting identified and expressed needs. This book is not a 'how to' guide for facilitating empowerment, but empowerment should underpin everything we do, including the gathering of evidence.

If our main purpose is seeing whether what we have done has impact, we need to know how to measure and assess the impact of community empowerment.

Longitudinal measures, as described in Chapters 10 and 12, are important, and choices about which dimensions of community empowerment should be measured or assessed are also important. It is not possible, we suggest, to measure all dimensions at once. You may be interested in self-esteem, which can be assessed using statistics and stories, or you may be interested in democracy and voter turnout using secondary data. Whatever data or information you choose to use will need to be triangulated and constructed into a multifaceted tower of evidence to illustrate community empowerment.

Power dynamics affect what we do and should be explicitly addressed in our work as community practitioners in gathering evidence, as the following example illustrates.

> Gerald works at a food bank in England and told us that practitioners who want to contact those who may be hard to reach often ask if they can come and meet people at the food bank for research and evaluation purposes. Gerald says no, they cannot do this, as it is a safe place for many people, including homeless people who need a place where they can just be themselves. Gerald himself is able to refer the homeless people to others if necessary and works hard to build their self-esteem.

We think Gerald is right to protect the space and to work with helping people to find their own way to be empowered. It is often difficult for homeless people to retain self-esteem, and there can be stigma associated with using a food bank. Sometimes people become tired and downtrodden and need space to be themselves. It is at this point that advocacy becomes important. When people cannot speak for themselves, speaking for and with them can be crucial to improving their situation and their wellbeing.

Power may reside in the individual practitioner who does not choose to empower participants and clients. It may also reside in systems and structures, in rules and regulations that distance people from the participants, in society and the culture that surrounds us, and in the attitudes and narratives of a community.

Karen worked in a town in Australia that had a narrative of being a town that was a good place to live. People were well off; tourists visited its beautiful beaches; and it had a good university, with lots of wealthy overseas students. Karen found there was some hidden poverty. It was, however, a town with another side. This narrative of the town was hard to bear for those who were poor and the town did not attract government funding to alleviate poverty because of its positive reputation. The narrative needed to change and the community needed to acknowledge that the town was not a place of wellbeing for all its citizens. It needed to empower those who were disadvantaged.

Jason worked for a local government housing office in Scotland. He often met people who were distraught or angry about their living conditions. This made him feel nervous, so he became very familiar with the systems and regulations that helped him to answer any questions or address complaints with a clear policy statement about what the council could or could not do with its budgets. People seemed to find this distressing, but it meant they often went away. Jason was probably in the wrong job and not supported appropriately, so used the systems to disempower people who were distressed. It made him able to cope. Jason finally left the job.

Ronan worked for a telephone-based helpline for older people who needed support with living alone. He was not used to working with elderly people, so he called the women 'my love' and told them everything would soon be 'tickety-boo' now that he was on the case. He was surprised that some of the older women found this inappropriate. He was using a power dynamic that is part of many cultures where women, particularly older women, are patronised and treated in a way that would be unacceptable for a man. He was well meaning, but got it wrong.

All of these examples show how people can become disempowered and how we can change our behaviour to avoid this happening. It is important in our work of gathering evidence that we are careful not to contribute to disempowerment. In each of the cases, the participants or clients are treated in a way that makes them powerless. All of the examples, but the first one in particular, lead us to consider the voice of participants and how people can be heard.

Voice

Having a voice is having both a presence and the agency to affect one's own wellbeing. People who are not heard are often referred to as 'hard to reach', but this is not necessarily the case as they are often easy to reach by people from the same community or background. It is important also not to 'other' people by lumping them together as 'the homeless' or 'the disempowered'. Yes, this may be the case, but it implies that people in these situations are the problem when society may be at fault. It also suggests that such people are different from everyone else in the community, which is not necessarily the case. Finally, it removes the humanity from these people, when in fact they are all as different individually as you and I. People we may think of as disempowered are often highly empowered in parts of their lives we do not see or we take for granted, as parents, for instance, or as a son or daughter.

It is, however, the case, that the people we choose to work with may be seldom heard by decision makers and practitioners. When we are gathering evidence, it is therefore crucial that what is heard is the authentic voice of our participants. We shall refer to clients, customers and participants as participants from now on, as this word, we suggest, is the least encumbered by power associations.

Voice is important, as it embraces how people choose to frame their experiences. Voice can very easily be manipulated in gathering evidence. Traditional interviews frame the subjects and concepts that are discussed. In Chapter 6, we discuss how this can be avoided using anecdote and storytelling. It is really quite easy to manipulate people to report what you want them to say about a project, and it is similarly easy to manipulate data by being selective, to show how what has been done has worked. This is dishonest on two counts. The first count is that it means the voice of the participants is inauthentic. The second count is that it denies the participants the opportunity to say what they think. We need to be both honest and authentic in the ways in which we seek and present the voice of our participants, as they are often rarely heard and need to be heard in the way that they choose to express their opinions. Interviews often ask people to conceptualise about ideas like confidence and self-esteem. This is wholly artificial for many people who would not choose to discuss these ideas naturally or would prefer to discuss concrete examples. In gathering evidence, we often ask people to speak like us for our purposes when instead we should be finding more naturalistic ways of seeking the voice that is rarely heard. This is discussed further in Chapter 9.

There is another dimension to voice, and that is finding the people who are rarely or seldom heard. It is often easy to go into a community and find people who will offer an opinion about just about anything you care to ask them. This, however, runs counter to the values of equality and inclusion. There is a perennial difficulty in deciding who speaks for a community. Often, in our experience, those who speak for a community speak for a selected vocal and more empowered part of the community. We consider it is inappropriate to suggest that any small group of people is representative of a community in qualitative data gathering. This causes difficulties with consultation. We need to work hard at consultation, as those who will come to a public meeting to comment on a planning proposal are not necessarily representative. They may be convenient as a sounding board, but they do not represent the needs, wants and desires of a whole community. We need to go out and find the people who will not come to public meetings. This means using networks of community workers, door knocking, visiting doctors' surgeries, for example, and developing trust. This takes time but is the only authentic method of consulting a community.

It is important to represent the voice of participants accurately by being clear about the context of any quotations used and not being so selective as to distort the voice. It is also crucial to think about how participants can express their own voice through participating in conferences, presentations and the writing-up of our work. Voice is much more than what is said; it is about the presence in a democracy of multiple views and the presence of people from all walks of life.

Trust

Honesty in consultation and evidence gathering is closely linked to trust, and definitions of trust in the dictionary include references to confidence that future relationships will be positive. Relationships are complex, and we have already discussed the power dynamics in relationships. Building trust is crucial to gathering authentic evidence of impact. People will tell you honestly about impact if they trust you. Trust is arguably more difficult for those working in the public sector to generate, as there is an implicit contract in the relationship – that is, they have a service to provide to a participant or community. The individual worker is also often backed by an edifice of bureaucracy that is disempowering for the participant. This is perhaps also true, but less the case, for practitioners working in the third sector who may be volunteers and where the contract is less formal and there may be less bureaucracy.

Building trust takes time, but it is well worth the time investment. There are many ways to build trust and many activities that can be initiated to get to know a community and begin the relationship. Trust relies on a relationship in which the community has confidence in the practitioner and can rely on practitioners doing what they say they will do, and in which confidences are not broken, and promises are fulfilled.

Community engagement

Engaging with a community is crucial in community work and is fundamental to building trust. Networking and befriending are, in turn, crucial to community engagement. People may choose not to attend events because of practical reasons, such as transport issues or lack of childcare. They may also choose not to attend because they are disaffected from society having low confidence or self-esteem. Snowballing is a useful technique for finding those who are seldom heard. This involves finding one person and asking them to bring a friend to an event; then asking the friend to bring another friend. This provides peer support for the individuals and will find people who might otherwise not participate in your activity. Door knocking is another technique that cannot be dismissed, although it may be threatening to some older people or those living on their own. Community engagement takes time and is founded on building trust, which means being always open and honest about your intentions and slowly forming a relationship with those who are seldom heard. Building trust takes time and can be difficult in societies where performance is measured on outputs such as the number of people involved in an activity. It is important, as the first step to community work, and we need better performance measures from managers to ensure trust building is valued as an important first step.

Participation

> Participation raises the likelihood that research questions and designs will be more responsive to community needs; that research executions will be more accurate in capturing community nuances; and that community members, having been brought into the research enterprise, will be more likely to pay attention to, agree with, and implement the recommendations of the research findings. (Jason et al, 2006, p xvii)

We have discussed power and its importance to working in the community. Gathering evidence of effectiveness frequently involves using research methods or techniques at the more formal end of the evidence continuum introduced in Chapter 1. Research in any form has a power dynamic that places the researcher above the respondent in an evidence-gathering context. The researcher is highly valued culturally and has the role of framing what is asked, discovered and known. She or he may also be more educated or more highly paid than those who are participating in the research. It is for these reasons that we value highly participatory approaches to evidence gathering. Individuals and the community are experts about what they have experienced in an intervention or activity. We are of the view that all people are capable of participating in research at many levels. Most individuals with appropriate support are capable of planning, designing and implementing research processes. The research findings may not be as polished, but they will be authentic.

A research project that looked at the experiences of people living in a geographical community and participating in the local government's adult learning programmes was undertaken in Scotland in 2018. A group of ten volunteers, identified through local geographical networks, was formed, and these people, with no prior knowledge of research, were trained in research processes and methods, including running focus groups and semi-structured interviews. They conducted interviews with key community figures who would be knowledgeable about the local area. The volunteers knew who to interview and chose publicans, teachers and historians as their sample through local knowledge. They were able to conduct focus groups locally through personal networks, avoiding interviewing the 'usual suspects'. The research reached seldom-heard people and contributed to changes to approaches in adult learning and a raising of the awareness of hidden poverty in the area. The volunteers were local experts and were well able, with support, to contribute to the research design and implementation. The advantages were that seldom-heard participants were reached and that local knowledge informed the research process.

This example shows how participation in the research process by those with local knowledge and experience can contribute to the content and quality of practitioners' findings. It is also a democratic process to include others in the research, as ten heads are better than one. It is also consistent with values of equality and inclusion to enable people to participate in research work. The quality of data may not be as 'sweet' and professional as that gathered solely by practitioners, but it will be authentic. We are of the opinion that everyone can gather evidence of effectiveness or do research and evaluation, if supported to do so.

It is important to include not only participants but also all stakeholders in the process of gathering evidence, so that all those who feel they have ownership are respected and informed. Stakeholders are also often gatekeepers to evidence. Box 2.2 introduces a useful resource for finding out more about participatory research.

Box 2.2 Further reading on community-based participatory research

Centre for Social Justice and Community Action and National Co-ordinating Centre for Public Engagement (2012) *Community-Based Participatory Research: A Guide to Ethical Principles and Practice*, Durham and Bristol: Centre for Social Justice and Community Action, Durham University, and National Co-ordinating Centre for Public Engagement, available at: www.dur.ac.uk/resources/beacon/ CBPREthicsGuidewebNovember 20121.pdf

---

Quality

We have used the term 'authentic' in referring to evidence or data in our research or finding-out processes, and this is deliberate as it is one measure of the quality of our findings. Quality of evidence is important, as it needs to be convincing and genuine. We would all prefer our evidence to be strong rather than weak. The word authentic means not only genuine, but also true, bona fide, reliable, dependable, honest, trustworthy, faithful and accurate.

Generalisability is often cited as one of the advantages of quantitative data. It is important, however, to think about the 'transferability' of qualitative data from one context to another. Often common sense tells us that if the circumstances or context are similar, qualitative data from one situation will apply in the other situation. We would, of course, need to check this, but we can make common-sense extrapolations about probability from qualitative data.

Quality has many dimensions, but we believe that authenticity is the most important factor in determining the quality of our evidence. If we are using statistical methods, the 'holy trinity' of reliability, reproducibility and generalisability is often applied, but it is our view that statistics and stories make the strongest evidence and a qualitative dimension demands authenticity. Measuring change is not possible in a community context without redress to the way it makes people think or feel. Statistics are, however, important in thinking about value for money and cost-effectiveness, but this is not the only dimension that we consider to be important in our work with people in communities. Quality criteria in research are a source of continuing academic debate but Tracy (2010) has sought to provide a comprehensive and all-encompassing set of criteria for qualitative research that we find helpful in its inclusiveness albeit not quite so helpful in its complexity. It is summarised here to help you look for quality in your evidence.

Tracy proposes that high-quality qualitative research is marked by:

- worthy topic
- rich rigour
- sincerity
- credibility
- resonance
- significant contribution
- ethics
- meaningful coherence

This once again brings us straight back to values. One person's idea of sincerity or credibility may be different from another person's idea. A significant contribution in action research of selected individuals in one context may be quite different from a significant contribution in the form of findings of a large number of semi-structured interviews. A worthy topic is relevant, timely, significant and interesting or evocative, according to Tracy, but another person's idea of evocative may be quite different from mine. Worthy to me means that it will make a difference to people's lives. Rich rigour is interesting as a criterion of quality. I prefer to use the word 'robust', as this has for me the connotations of strong and freshly brewed coffee or sturdiness, as described in Chapter 1. Sincerity is important because, as mentioned previously, weaker evidence discarded in traditional research may still be used in evidence gathering. Using triangulation or cumulatively using evidence that may appear weaker may be very important (McArdle, 2018).

Hermeneutics

Hermeneutics denotes meanings, and we are concerned with it here as it can make our evidence stronger than it might otherwise be. When we generate evidence, we can transform it through making meaning from it.

A project was run in Australia with people who misused substances such as alcohol and drugs. The project used holistic techniques of yoga, spiritual awareness and mindfulness to assist people to remain off the drugs and alcohol. This was evaluated by asking participants to tell their stories from when they first heard about the project to the time when the project finished. Colourful stories emerged of offending (shoplifting) ceasing; of family reunions without the former problems of alcohol getting in the way; of feeling better about oneself and gaining in confidence to try attending other classes. The evaluator had many strong stories to show the funders about the fact that the project had had a positive influence on individuals' behaviour but the researcher looked for what brought these stories together and why yoga and the other elements had worked, and was able to point to a change in identity over the period of the project. People had a new way of thinking about self in terms of mind, body and spirit that required that they look at the whole of themselves and figure out what made alcohol or drug abuse happen in the first place; what the triggers were; and what made participants feel good about themselves. How the project worked was a stronger message for the funders than the fact that a holistic and alternative project worked, and this would put this project higher up the list of likely funded projects when money is limited.

Meaning making involves having sufficient evidence to make comparisons and reading between the lines of interviews or focus groups. Data analysis and interpretation lead to meaning making. We have to look for what is implied or not said, as well as what is said. Sometimes evidence can be a little rough and we need to derive meaning from it to make it count. Working with children, in particular, often demands skills of seeing what is not said and deriving meaning from it, or interpreting drawings and pictures. Put simply, we need to look below the surface of the evidence we gather and see what it tells us about people and the service or experience they have had.

In Part II of this book, we focus on the 'how to' dimensions of gathering evidence and present a wide range of methods of doing so. The values that underpin your work as a practitioner will underpin how you go about gathering evidence of the impact of change and the kind of evidence you collect, so it may be useful to spend a little time thinking about the following challenge questions, and your answers to them, to clarify your values.

Challenge questions

1. Why are you engaged in work in the community?
2. What are your deeply held beliefs about equality, inclusion and social justice?

3. What for you are the important dimensions of community empowerment?
4. How does your sex, gender and ethnicity affect the work you do in gathering evidence and more generally in the work you do?
5. Have you encountered any ethical dilemmas when gathering evidence? If so, did you resolve them, and how did you do so?

References

Berger, R. (2013) Now I see it, now I don't: researcher's position and reflexivity in qualitative research, *Qualitative Research*, 15(2): 219–34.

Brinkmann, S. and Kvale, S. (2015) *Interviews: Learning the Craft of Qualitative Research Interviewing*, Thousand Oaks, CA: Sage.

Driver, J. (2007) *Ethics: The Fundamentals*, Oxford: Blackwell.

Foucault, M. (1990) *The Will to Knowledge: The History of Sexuality: Volume 1* (trans. Robert Hurley), London: Penguin.

Israel, B.A., Checkoway, B., Schulz, A. and Zimmerman, M. (1994) Health education and community empowerment: conceptualising and measuring perceptions of individual, organizational and community control, *Health Education Quarterly*, 21(2): 149–70.

Jason, L., Keys, C., Suarez-Balcazer, Y., Taylor, R. and Davis, M. (2006) *Participatory Community Research: Theories and Methods in Action*, Washington, DC: American Psychological Association.

Laverack, G. (2006) Improving health outcomes through community empowerment: a review of the literature, *Journal of Health, Population and Nutrition*, 24(1): 113–20.

McArdle, K. (2018) *Freedom Research in Education: Becoming an Autonomous Researcher*, Basingstoke: Palgrave Macmillan.

McArdle, K. Hurrell, A. and Muñoz Martinez, Y. (2013) What makes teachers good at what they do? The axiological model, in J. McNiff (ed) *Value and Virtue in Practice-Based Research*, Poole: September Books, pp 79–92.

Pring, R. (2004) *Philosophy of Education: Aims, Theory, Common Sense and Research*, London: Continuum.

Ransome, P. (2013) *Ethics and Values in Social Research*, Basingstoke: Palgrave Macmillan.

Tracy, S.J. (2010) Qualitative quality: eight "big-tent" criteria for excellent qualitative research, *Qualitative Inquiry*, 16(10): 837–51.

3

A challenging context in which values matter

Karen McArdle

Introduction

As professionals, not only do we work in complex and sometimes demanding community roles but also sometimes in challenging contexts in which we seek to generate evidence of impact. These challenges come from a range of sources and require us to have a means of dealing with them. This chapter introduces the social context in which many of us work and considers the means of dealing with challenges. We consider in this chapter the different kinds of knowing that we can use in gathering evidence, the ways in which values underpin this knowing and the impact of this on the evidence we present to others. The power of knowledge is discussed in different domains alongside its importance in the process of gathering evidence.

Challenges in the social professions

For each of us, the social context will be different and will depend on the culture of our country, our location in that country, the culture of our organisation or profession, and the experiences we have of our team or colleagues and of our supervisor or manager. It will also depend on the character and history of our participants. There are, however, arguably a range of factors that influence our experience of work that are common across social professions. It is important here to introduce the notion of history, and the idea that it lingers with us longer than we necessarily need it and it is imbued in all of us. Much is written about history and how it affects individuals. Arguably, the most commonly referenced ideas are those of Pierre Bourdieu (1977 [1972]), who used the term 'habitus' to refer to 'second nature'. Bourdieu describes how the unconscious operates in the following way:

> The 'unconscious' is never anything other than the forgetting of history, which history itself produces by incorporating the objective structures it produces in the second natures of 'habitus' … in each of us in varying proportions there is part of yesterday's man [sic]; it is yesterday's man who inevitably predominates in us, since the present amounts to little compared with the long past in the course of which we were formed and from which we result. Yet we do not sense this man of the past, because he is inveterate in us; he makes up the unconscious part of ourselves. (1977 [1972], p 79)

One can be very aware of recent history because it has not had time to become part of our unconscious, but there are older histories that form our dispositions. In short, the habitus mentioned by Bourdieu produces individual and collective practices that seem sensible and reasonable but are the product of our individual and collective histories. The history of rural communities, for example, informs, in subtle ways, how people in communities react today. One of the common side effects of this 'habitus' is the fact that people may behave in ways that are relevant to the past, and all that this imbues, without necessarily realising that this is relevant to a historical context and may not be relevant today. So in the example given in Chapter 1 of fishing communities in rural Scotland, the history of such communities, imbued with a downturn in the fishing industry and fear of outsiders, is such that the residents may be suspicious of well-intentioned interventions to support the community in the current economic climate. Historical events have had a negative effect on the way of life of these communities. We shall return to this later in the chapter when we discuss organisational culture.

Drawing on their experience, Fook and Gardner (2007) discuss some of the challenges faced by professionals today, largely in the context of the social work profession, but we argue that these challenges are transferable to other contexts. Common issues, derived from Fook and Gardner (2007), include:

- a sense of powerlessness linked to uncertainty;
- fear or risk of being wrong;
- increased social and economic complexity.

Common organisational responses, again derived and adapted from Fook and Gardner (2007), include:

- pressure to work to rules and procedures;
- paperwork;
- focus on the parts or detail rather than the whole;
- a focus on inputs and outputs, rather than quality.

The sense of powerlessness mentioned here concerns decisions being made without consultation. Increasing uncertainty about job futures is exacerbated as organisations restructure and change. Restructuring is a very common response to change management, in big organisations in particular, but this can be disempowering and worrying for staff.

A fear or risk of being wrong is linked to the sense of responsibility arising from working with people and the need to 'get it right' first time, as community work concerns people's lives. This arguably goes with the territory of working with people and communities, but, in some social professions, there is the fear and risk of being publicly vilified over one's actions if they are perceived to be, or indeed are, 'wrong'.

Increased economic and social complexity refers to social change such as the austerity measures present in countries where government seeks to make savings by cutting services and associated jobs. In particular, services that carry no statutory obligation come under threat, such as libraries, music tuition in schools and other worthwhile and important services. The social complexity mentioned here refers to societal change in family structures; for example, increased social isolation is an issue in many rural and urban communities in the UK as the age profile of residents increases and younger families move to follow jobs.

You may recognise some of the resultant organisational responses. It is our view that many organisations are stuck in history, in a 'modernist' tradition based on the manufacturing and factories of the industrial revolution, where inputs and outputs are calculated and effectiveness is based on performance indicators that can be measured rather than qualitative measures that concern the quality of people's lives. In a postmodern context, organisations can choose to be more flexible and more engaged with local and personal knowledge of successes in the community. Pressure to work to rules and procedures is a response to risk and reflects the organisation's need for safety. Rules and procedures can be important, but can also be limiting. The other organisational responses are similarly a response to fear of risk and the desire for control in a challenging context.

This is not a book about organisational development, however, but one that concerns itself with how professionals continually develop knowledge and practice in a changing and complex context. In this book, we are concerned with the knowledge that leads to evidence of good practice. The social context of organisations is not immutable and individuals can contribute to their change in ways within their compass. We return to this later in the chapter when we discuss reflection and reflexivity. We now turn to ways of knowing in this complex environment and how they are valued.

Epistemological considerations

Epistemology is the study of ways of knowing. We can know things in different ways; we can believe them, trust them, feel them and see them, as well as know them. Knowledge is affected by social considerations; there is a power dynamic that accompanies certain ways of knowing. The Western press is really interested in quantitative data that are largely causal, for example. So stories about lead pollution causing a child's death, or studies that show how what we eat causes cancer, are of interest to the press.

So, too, politicians tend to be interested in quantitative data, generally in the accessible form of percentages, and, again, causality and a degree of representativeness to bigger populations. Quantitative data can be presented in straightforward and accessible ways, and link cause to outcome. Many politicians do like to hear the voice of participants, but this is the exception rather than the rule. In some countries, particularly developing countries, the perceived certainty of quantitative information is preferred in many professions over qualitative studies. One Indonesian colleague, for example, doing sound action research on medical education, found convincing colleagues of its value to be a challenge. So data that is not in this quantitative form can be excluded from public exposure at the expense of causal data that provide reassurance of the ability to act to control the cause. The simplicity of such data is reassuring over the management of complexity that is required in more qualitative studies.

Accordingly, knowledge is imbued with power and status, and comes in different forms. It is important in gathering evidence of effectiveness to be aware of this power and status and its impact on many behaviours and choices. Cognitive knowledge, which may be seen as facts and critical thinking, is the bedrock of many higher educational institutions, for example, so students are admitted, taught and assessed in the cognitive domain in many cases and their success will depend to an extent on their ability to manage this form of knowledge.

There are many different ways of knowing and they carry different power and status. It is important to recognise these, as there will be ways in which you can know the impact of what you do that differ from the more traditional qualitative and quantitative methods that are commonly described in books about evaluation. There are ways we can know that are quite obvious. We can know from memory or perception, for example, but there are ways we can know from practice that lend themselves to the processes of gathering evidence. It is difficult to be exhaustive about ways of knowing, but the following example from the medical profession illustrates this panoply.

Thinking about epistemology and student doctors, we identified the following ways of knowing for health professionals:

Among other things, they can know through:

- cognition/problem solving/reasoning – knowing how to diagnose illness;
- authority, experts – knowing the literature on the causes of illness;
- experience/practice/touch/smell/feel – the practice of managing similar illnesses;
- emotion – 'this illness is worrying';
- aesthetics – 'this looks a very bad case';
- imagination – 'what if I treated it like this?';
- ethics, values – 'what is the best treatment for this patient's situation?';
- intuition – 'I know this is likely to work';
- history/tradition/culture – 'this has traditionally been the known approach';
- common sense – 'it makes practical sense to do this';
- interrelationships (for example, authority/experience) – 'my colleague did this successfully the other day'.

You may be able to add to this list in terms of knowing for your profession or for the health profession. Finding a definition of knowledge is difficult as there are different kinds of knowledge – it is a family resemblance concept like the term 'games'. Games are different and it is hard to find a definition that will cover all games, but most of us recognise a game when we come across it.

There are orthodoxies about the way one knows in different circles. For example, in educational community work, experiential learning is highly valued. In the health profession, however, randomised controlled trials are valued. When thinking about orthodoxies, it is important to challenge them and to think about who it is that maintains this is the way to be and whether it is justified. Why is one way of knowing valued over others? For example, in academic circles, the valued knowledge in the past has been cognitive and the means of teaching it has been transmission from expert to student. This still occurs sometimes and is a concrete means of maintaining authority and power. It is justified, arguably, in transmitting propositional knowledge or fact, but not all knowledge comes in this form. You might think about your own profession and where the knowledge comes from; what kind of knowledge it is; who maintains it; and how it is maintained. Should it be challenged? Think about the knowledge that is required in your profession to show effectiveness and impact. What kind of knowledge is it? Can it be justified? How could it be extended?

For community workers, knowledge is often local, anecdotal and historical, and these forms of knowing are not always highly valued, which implies a need to argue their relevance and importance to our work and to convert these forms of knowing into strong evidence of impact. Here we outline how to do this.

While we know things in many ways, as suggested in the earlier health example, knowledge has traditionally been seen as involving justification. Knowledge always consists of justified, true belief. If we want to assert something is true and if we want to have true beliefs, we must have justification (O'Brien, 2017). This is clearly necessary if we are asserting our belief that what we do is important and effective and has impact. We need justification. In this context, justification consists of evidence and argument. We need this belief ourselves and need to justify this belief to others. Chapter 4 on presentation takes these ideas further.

Validating knowledge claims is not a mechanical process, but is instead argumentative practice (Polkinghorne, 2007). We need when presenting evidence to anticipate and think about the response we would have to questions from our audience or readers. Polkinghorne (2007) suggests we need to answer these questions in our presentation. We need to cite our evidence, link the evidence to our conclusions about the value of what we have done, and ensure that these conclusions are persuasive. One means of ensuring that conclusions are persuasive is through the use of reflexivity and being explicit about this. Reflexivity is introduced later in this chapter, but first we consider the role of reflective practice.

Knowing in a complex and changing environment

The most important process of knowing in a complex and changing environment is through reflection. Reflection is thinking about our practice in a particular way. Many of the social professions build their models of continuing professional development on reflective practice. Reflection is a much-contested term and its application in practice can be difficult in terms of how to actually do it (McArdle, 2018). It is our experience that reflective practice in a busy environment can fall by the wayside. Reflective practice is, however, the main means of dealing with complexity and change. This is because it gives us the space to process complexity and to synthesise ideas, so that we can make good judgements about our action, responding as best we can to the complexity that surrounds us and use all our ways of knowing in forming opinions and making choices.

Fook and Gardner (2007) define the method of critical reflection that we believe can make a difference to both society and the individual's practice. Clearly, reflection is about thinking, but it is more than this.

> It involves a deeper look at the premises on which, thinking, action and emotions are based. It is critical when connections are made between these assumptions and the social world as a basis for change. (Fook and Gardner, 2007, p 15)

The key points are the understanding of self in a social context; challenging assumptions; and linking a changed way of thinking to changed actions. Reflective practice has the potential to effect change in society as well as in the individual. Our changed actions can affect the world in which we live. It is in principle about unearthing taken-for-granted assumptions.

There is limited agreement in the literature and among professionals about how exactly one should reflect. We consider it is best done in a face-to-face setting, with one or more trusted people, to tackle assumptions behind what has or can be done. It involves, we suggest:

- exploring critical incidents;
- looking at the social context of these incidents;
- exploring and dealing with the emotions associated with these incidents;
- challenging ideas about what is or should be;
- seeking means of improving practice;
- improving practice.

We know people who have a cup of coffee and a bit of a think about things and claim they are reflecting. This is not the case; reflection is about being uncomfortable and needs to be critical. Much has been written over the years since Donald Schön's seminal work (1987) on reflective practice.

> The purpose of reflection is to confuse, disarrange and thereby become awakened. (Ekebergh, 2009, p 52)

Reflective practice involves asking challenging questions and seeking alternative actions. The following dialogue illustrates a situation described by Karen during a reflective conversation with a trusted friend, Clare, who has taken on the role of mentor.

Karen: 'I ran a group training session on research methods. It was supposed to have ten people but only four turned up and I felt it was rather flat and unexciting. The people reported to the organiser, who evaluated it that it was good but it troubles me now two weeks after the event that I did not make it as lively and exciting as it could have been.'

Clare: 'What is it about you that requires every event to be 'lively and exciting'? It seems that the participants found it fine.'

Karen: 'I like to do a good job for everyone.'

Clare: 'But they said you did do a good job. Why are you putting your opinion above the opinion of the participants?'

Karen: 'Fair point. I guess I am used to doing these workshops and consider myself to be a bit of an expert.'

Clare: 'How about using the feedback more explicitly and judging yourself in this context rather than according to your own terms.'

Karen: 'Thanks. I shall do this next time.'

In this short piece, Clare was challenging and helped Karen to see that her opinion was unbalanced and, most importantly, Clare found a way to lead to action that is different in a similar situation. Often reflection is about assumptions and these are based on deeply held beliefs about the world and self in the world. The conversation above could have taken a different and equally valid path after Karen outlined the problem to Clare, as outlined in the following example.

Clare: 'What is it about you, Karen, that requires that every session is perfect? The participants said it was fine. Are you a perfectionist?'

Karen: 'Well, I suppose I set high standards for myself all the time.'

Clare: 'Why is that?'

Karen: 'Well, I guess I always want to be the best at what I do.'

Clare: 'Where does that come from?'

Karen: 'Well, I suppose I've always been like that since I was a child. My parents had high, very high expectations of what I should achieve in everything and I guess that lives with me now.'

Clare: 'Well it clearly causes you some stress, as you are concerned two weeks after the event about something that was good but not perfect. How about accepting "good" and working with the participants to see if they indeed missed what you think was missing?'

It is important to reflect on action, but in a way that challenges and is not too safe. There is a place for safe conversations, but these are not necessarily reflection. In helping others, it is important to take on the role of mentor or critical friend to support others in challenging their own assumptions. It is a way in which we can learn in a complex and changing environment – only one of many ways we can learn, but arguably the most important and accessible.

Going back to the thinking about organisational development, it is important to be aware that a learning organisation is made up of individual learners and a learning culture is important to the quality of what is done in a service or project. Managers should support and value critical reflection. Chapter 6, on anecdote and observation, discusses the use of reflective material as evidence.

Reflexivity

Reflexivity is the process of looking back over what one has done, of gathering evidence to see how one's own values, beliefs, opinions and activities have affected what has been done. At its simplest, it might involve checking whether we have used leading questions in interviews or evaluations. At a deeper level, it concerns how we frame an inquiry to discover its impact on participants, for example, what have we chosen to include or exclude in our frame of reference for the inquiry.

Bolton (2014, p 7) provides the following helpful definition of reflexivity:

> To be reflexive is to examine. For example, the limits of our knowledge, how our own behavior plays into organisational structures counter to our own personal and professional values, and why such practices might marginalise groups or exclude individuals. It is questioning how congruent our actions are with our espoused values and theories….

There are common ways to be reflexive in an inquiry. These include using the inquiry instrument on yourself, so filling in a questionnaire yourself, or being interviewed yourself with your questions to see what your assumptions are. This can be very illuminating and surprising. Another way to be reflexive is to keep a reflexive diary of your thoughts and opinions over the process of the inquiry and how you interpret, in particular, your findings. A third way of being reflexive is to have a mentor to ask you challenging questions about your impact on the inquiry you are conducting. A fourth way of being reflexive is to analyse your reflective diary as if it were research data and see what assumptions you have made about the way the world is or should be.

Facts or data are the results and constructions of our own interpretation of what we have found out (Alvesson and Skoldberg, 2000). They are not objective things that are true. Reflexivity is the capacity of the researcher to be aware of his/her own thoughts, feelings, culture, environment and social and personal history in representing what she or he has chosen to find out (Etherington, 2004). Like reflection, reflexivity is intended to be a bit uncomfortable. Dean (2014) refers to the metacognitive processes of reflexivity, reflecting back on past learning, and sees it as thinking about thinking; learning about learning; and reflection on reflection.

Reflexivity, as mentioned earlier in this chapter, can be used as a means of persuasion or showing the validity of what has been done to gather evidence. Reflexivity can be used in a major way to show that bias has not affected what we assert in our presentation of evidence. We can show through reflexivity what our assumptions have or have not been and how we have been honest and truthful in our report of our work.

Self-awareness and values

Reflection and reflexivity are not value-free (McArdle, 2018), but are founded on strong, coherent, ethical principles and values about the way professionals should behave. We need to be aware of the values we hold and how these affect the way in which we see, interpret and present the impact of what we do. Remember the importance of justification of our beliefs mentioned earlier in this chapter. Self-evaluation is discussed in more detail in Chapter 15, but, here in thinking about reflection and reflexivity, we need to be conscious of the link to self-evaluation. Reflection, reflexivity and self-evaluation demand the need for self-awareness.

There are many books and courses that seek to enhance our self-awareness. In this context, we need to think about it in terms of its relationship to our effectiveness. We need to know our own strengths and limitations, and also our own boundaries and areas of comfort in work. We need to know this so that we can be sure we can justify our beliefs in the form of the evidence of impact we choose to use. We are of the view that being self-aware is not an end point; rather, it is something we should strive for continually, as values are modified and change in a complex and changing world. Also, we do not always act according to our value base. Karen can think of times when she has felt uncomfortable with her research or practice, and analysing the source of the discomfort has led her to conclude that she did not include others as much as she would ideally choose in terms of the values of inclusion and equality. Discomfort is often a sure sign of value conflict.

Values are our deeply held beliefs and are far from immutable. They affect what we do, how we do it and with whom. This matters when we are explaining the impact of what we do. We may have things that we consider to be 'non-negotiable'; these are usually values. Gelb (1998) suggests our goals answer the questions 'What do I want?', whereas the question 'How much do I want it?' is a question of values. As one thinks about deeper motivations, core values emerge.

What is intrinsically valuable is the subject of philosophical discourse but may include knowledge, pleasure, beauty, loving relationships, health and virtue (Schafer-Landau, 2007). We use value talk all the time, using evaluative expressions such as good, bad, better, best, great, fine, excellent, poor and terrible. We suggest that there is no such thing as objective values (Mackie, 2007); they are always subjective and the product of our history our culture and our character. For example, by interpreting social practices, rituals and internal conflicts, we can understand a community's unspoken and unwritten values and norms (Orsi, 2015). We should apply this to ourselves and our organisations. The norms and values we hold determine what we do and hence our impact or lack of it on our participants and on our funders, stakeholders and managers.

Intrinsically good activities are, arguably, seeking others' wellbeing or society's wellbeing. There is a long tradition of thinking philosophically about what is good or constitutes wellbeing. In the context of gathering evidence of what is good about our work, we need to think about what exactly good or wellbeing means to us. It can clearly be different for different people. What constitutes the good for society differs depending on where you stand in politics. Are you left-wing or right-wing in your beliefs? Similarly, wellbeing for the individual is making a moral judgement about what is best for them, even if it is the case that you believe the individual should decide for themselves. Values underpin all that we choose to do. They may be our values or the values of our profession or organisation, and an awareness of these values is vital to understanding what impact we choose to have and, therefore, whether the impact exists.

Our values and beliefs underpin how we communicate our work to others. If we believe in an observable and measurable reality, we shall probably be descriptive of our work and participants, and use language that is factual and allows general application of the work we do. If, however, we believe a given reality is different for each person who perceives or experiences it, we shall probably communicate the opinion of our participants and refer to them as individuals. Furthermore, how we value our participants will determine whether we choose to include them, by having relevant and accessible reporting methods. If we believe that employment is a 'good thing' for all people and for society as a whole, this will determine how we present our work with young people post-school age. We shall probably present employment destinations or college or further study. If we believe young people should choose freely their destination post-school, we shall present our findings differently and maybe emphasise positive relationships or arts-based achievement and volunteering instead.

Clearly, the values of the audience to whom we are presenting evidence will affect what we present. Taking the earlier employment example, if we are presenting to a government, which funds employability, we are likely to emphasise such outcomes, but if we are presenting to a philanthropic trust or charity, we may perceive them to be more open to the notion of wider, arts-based outcomes. We can, of course, seek to represent our values to others by presenting to government the value of outcomes that do not fall directly in its line of interest and persuade it of the inherent value of such alternative outcomes, but such a strategy is more risky in terms of satisfying funders that money has been well spent and needs careful argument.

Identifying the values that underpin what we do is helpful in seeking to show evidence of impact. It will assist us to choose what funding or projects we take on; how we implement them; and, accordingly, how they are valued in terms of outcomes that are valued by us and by other stakeholders, including funders.

This chapter has shown how knowledge, values, reflection and reflexivity are interrelated and have bearing on managing, and therefore showing, evidence of good practice in a complex environment. We suggest that the following challenge questions are particularly important in terms of a context for your thinking before proceeding with the methods in Part II.

Challenge questions

1. What do you consider to be your deeply held beliefs? From where do these beliefs come?
2. What are the values and assumptions that underpin your profession?
3. Are the values of your organisation in harmony or conflict with these expressed values?
4. What are the values of the policy makers or funders of your work?
5. How do your answers to these questions affect what you do?
6. How do the answers to these questions affect your presentation of evidence of impact?
7. When was the last time you genuinely reflected on your work?
8. What was the impact of this reflection on your subsequent action?

References

Alvesson, M. and Skoldberg, K. (2000) *Reflexive Methodology: New Vistas for Qualitative Research*, London: Sage.

Bolton, G. (2014) *Reflective Practice: Writing and Professional Development* (4th edn), London: Sage.

Bourdieu, P. (1977 [1972]) *Outline of a Theory of Practice* (trans. R. Nice), New York: Cambridge University Press.

Dean, C. (2014) How the process of doctoral enquiry developed my openness and criticality, Presentation at Fourth International Conference on Value and Virtue in Practice-Based Research, 21–23 July, St John University, York.

Ekebergh, M. (2009) Developing a didactic method that emphasizes lifeworld as a basis for learning, *Reflective Practice*, 10(1): 51-63.

Etherington, K. (2004) *Becoming a Reflexive Researcher: Using our Selves in Research*, London: Jessica Kingsley.

Fook, J. and Gardner, F. (2007) *Practising Critical Reflection: A Resource Handbook*, Maidenhead: Open University Press.

Gelb, M. (1998) *Think Like Da Vinci*, London: Harper Element.

Mackie, J.L. (2007) 'The subjectivity of values', in R. Schafer-Landau (ed) *Ethical Theory: An Anthology*, Oxford: Blackwell, pp 25–35.

McArdle, K. (2018) *Freedom Research in Education: Becoming an Autonomous Researcher*, Cham: Palgrave Macmillan.

O'Brien, D. (2017) *An Introduction to the Theory of Knowledge* (2nd edn), Cambridge: Polity Press.

Orsi, F. (2015) *Value Theory*, London: Bloomsbury.

Polkinghorne, E. (2007) Validity issues in narrative research, *Qualitative Inquiry*, 15(4): 471–486.

Schafer-Landau, R. (ed) (2007) *Ethical Theory: An Anthology*, Oxford: Blackwell.

Schön, D.A. (1984) *The Reflective Practitioner: How Professionals Think in Action*, New York, NY: Basic Books.

PART II

Methods of gathering evidence

The chapters in this section are intended to be read individually and in any order, although we recommend that you read Part I first, if you have not already done so, as this provides important context for the methods in Part II.

4

Presenting findings to different audiences

Catherine McKay and Karen McArdle

Introduction

You may be surprised to find that the first chapter in this part of the book is about presenting your findings. Usually, this topic appears at the end of a text, but we consider that presenting your findings is one of the first things you need to think about when expressing impact and when planning your project or services. There are particular complexities and challenges in working in community settings and it is not possible to simply undertake a project and then write it up with a quick evaluation, as the process is so much more complex and generating evidence needs careful planning from the very start. You will almost certainly also be generating multiple sources of evidence.

Increasingly, in times of austerity or rapid change, community work needs to present to decision makers and funders the effectiveness of what is funded and the impact of what is done. This is important to achieve sustainability of services; innovation in response to change; adaptation of services to meet new needs; and changes in service profile. It is also important for professional knowledge of the effectiveness of what we do – for self-evaluation. Finally, we have a responsibility to the communities with which we work, to share with them the impact of community work in order to celebrate successes and learn about what else can and needs to be done.

Presentation of findings can be done in many ways, too many to include all of them in this chapter, but we wish to encourage you to use your imagination and to find ways to include your participants in this process.

Planning your presentation

There are many approaches to planning a project, into which presentation must be built. One example is the Learning Evaluation and Planning (LEAP) framework, developed by the Scottish Community Development Centre, 2007. This method focuses on outcomes and partnership, and encourages practitioners to think about a series of questions that assist with planning and implementing their work. These questions focus on how you will achieve the difference you plan to make; how you will know you have made a difference; and how you can apply the lessons learned to future work. It links to the framework *How Good is the Learning and Development in Our Community?* (Education Scotland, 2016), which is both a useful self-evaluation tool and formal inspection framework for community learning and development in Scotland with a focus on partnership-based evaluation.

There are many ways in which we may undertake planning of projects. The key point we wish to make here is that, in community work, we need to build into the planning process the points (dates and stages) at which we intend to gather evidence, and the methods we intend use to do this. Presentation of findings will be determined by a number of factors, including dates and stages. The funder of the project may require a final summative report and specify the form of evaluation. Decision makers may need committee reports in a formal format. You may choose to celebrate the project through a final public meeting for participants. In all these examples, you need to plan into your process the dates and stages of sourcing of evidence and concomitant presentations. The following example shows what can be achieved through careful planning of evidence gathering and presentation.

A 12-week outdoor adult learning project was developed by the Forestry Commission in Scotland. The programme was designed for people accessing mental health services who wanted to make positive changes to their wellbeing through engagement with nature in a woodland setting. Activities included identifying different species of plants and wildlife; pond dipping; engaging in mindfulness; and taking part in woodland crafts, such as making charcoal.

At the end of each week of the programme, the partners involved in delivery reflected on what, from their perspective, did or did not go well and then time was set aside for the participants and practitioners to share their thoughts. During the first week, the participants were given a sketch book they could use to develop a journal of their experience, if they so wished.

The project was transformational in terms of mental health as shown by evidence of each of the participants achieving a John Muir Award (through a national environmental award scheme that encourages people to connect with, enjoy and care for wild places) and reporting increased feelings of self-confidence, self-worth and self-esteem. Individuals also progressed towards a positive destination of their choosing.

Presenting the findings of the project took many forms and was complex because of the range of organisations and professions involved in its delivery. As you would expect, each of the community workers evaluated the project according to their own organisation's internal reporting structures. However, in addition to this, the participants hosted a celebration and invited service managers from mental health and addiction fields into their woodland space, to share stories from their experiences of the project. The intention behind this was to provide a primary source of evidence of the project's efficacy to those able to influence future funding and encourage prospective participants. Evidence was also presented through a formal summative report that was disseminated to every agency involved in the project's delivery, along with a collaborative 'ezine'. The ezine was a culmination of photographs, journal pages and poetry reflecting participants' experiences during the course of the project, as recorded in their sketch books among other things. The ezine is designed to be left in community spaces where potential future participants may gather, such as community centres, doctors' waiting rooms and recovery cafés.

This case study shows the complexity of different stages at which evidence may be gathered and shows the imaginative ways in which it can be generated and used for both learning and for future recruitment and awareness raising.

Formality/informality

The ezine example was entirely appropriate for purpose. Presentations to funders are likely to be, but by no means definitely are, more formal. Decision makers may require formal written reports, but these need to be written accessibly, and formal does not equate with dry and boring. There may be routine information that must be included, but try to make the 'voice' of the community heard. Perhaps the funder would indeed like to see an ezine. Informality is often more attractive and authentic. Presenting findings through poetry, theatre and visual images can be very attractive and engaging. We urge you to try as far as is reasonably possible to be creative in your presentation about impact. Art-based methods are good for dealing with complexity and uncertainty, as they can communicate implicit as well as explicit meaning from a project.

> [A]cademic writing tends to draw on textual forms –
> tropes – which construct a god-like, all-seeing, all-
> knowing, all-comprehending stance, which is at the
> same time disinterested and fair. Real authors are, of
> course, located in history in particular communities,

constrained by their grasp (or lack of grasp) of bodies of ideas by the quality of their libraries and so on. Writing is full of serendipity and is inseparable from academic biography. (Potter, 2004, p 10)

This quotation is about academics but is relevant to the community worker and writer of reports. Avoid the 'god-like and all-seeing and all-knowing approach'. In our experience as practitioners, community workers often feel that reports should be written in a slightly unnatural way. They may, inappropriately in our view, overly rely on the passive voice ('the project was run') rather than using 'I' or 'we' statements ('we ran the project') and feel that the language needs to be complicated. We believe that the natural voice of the author is the best, the most convincing way to express impact. We also believe that impact is best communicated through introducing an element of the passion that goes with a job well done and impact/change achieved. Rather than trying to be too objective, try to inject some of your enthusiasm.

Miller and colleagues (2015) describe how poetry can introduce a third voice other than the interviewer or interviewee and suggest that it is a special language that can engage, reach and resonate with more diverse audiences. They studied residential care in Australia and produced a poem, part of which is reproduced below.

You Could Scream the Place Down

All your independence is taken away from you.
I'm not able to do it myself.
That's very hard to take,
you get so frustrated at times
you could scream the place down.
(Miller et al, 2015, p 410)

This poem expresses the frustration of an elderly woman through the use of repetition and rhythm, and the bluntness of her reality in the shortened lines. We believe it is good to consider creative approaches such as this to express what your participants wish to say.

Triple hermeneutic

Evidence may be linked to what Brinkmann and Kvale (2015) refer to as the 'triple hermeneutic'. Hermeneutics is simply the study of meaning. The triple hermeneutic has three elements. For example, the practitioner may gather evidence from an interviewee who has a meaning to express (first hermeneutic), then interpret this evidence (second hermeneutic) and write a story or report about it. The third hermeneutic comes into play when the reader makes sense of the story. It is important to think about our own interpretation of what people say to us about their experiences. Have we influenced what they say by who we are and how we asked a question? In terms of presentation and the third hermeneutic, we need to put ourselves in the readers' or listeners' shoes and see what they will make of what we present.

The most important decision when thinking about presentation of evidence is to consider the audience and what they will expect from you. Simple matters must be taken into account, such as the degree of formality or informality that will be expected and whether you can challenge expectations. You may well have more than one audience, such as funders and participants, and need to plan two forms of presentation, such as a report on the project's outcomes and outputs for the funders and, say, a leaflet for participants that summarises the findings in more simple language and ideas.

Regardless of the brevity and informality of a presentation, there are certain key elements that must be included in most presentations:

- the purpose or intention of the project/service;
- who was involved;
- what happened;
- what participants thought of it;
- the cost and resource implications;
- the extent to which the project met its stated purpose.

For more formal reports, expect to include the following:

- a title;
- a project summary of one page or less;
- a statement of aims and objectives;
- a description of the stakeholders;
- a description of the participants;
- a methods statement – or what was done and how;
- a description of the evidence gathered and the key findings of the evidence gathered;
- a statement of what the evidence reveals about the strengths and any limitations of the project;
- a financial statement of the funding available and the final project costs;
- conclusions and recommendations for the future;
- appendices if relevant – to include, for example, a sample of evidence or a sample of a letter of consent used for evidence gathering.

You will no doubt also include in a formal report any relevant secondary data or literature. See Chapter 14 for further guidance on secondary data.

The nature of your audience will help you determine the medium of the presentation. If your project was for young people who are technologically literate, a post or blog might be the best way to reach them, incorporating pictures and visual aids. The target audience will determine the complexity of ideas that you express. Most people can understand difficult concepts, so it is important not to underestimate them; just keep the language simple. Funding bodies are more likely than politicians to be willing to give time to complex arguments; the latter may prefer a summary.

The voice of participants

The voice of participants is crucial in presenting evidence of impact and has already been discussed in Part I. It is a form of empowerment and inclusion to ensure that their point of view is heard. They may be our clients, our learners or our patients, but their point of view is missing if not heard. To omit their perspective when evaluating something that they have experienced is to use and abuse a form of power. If participants find communicating difficult, there are often ways around this, for example, by involving family, carers and therapists. One of us, Karen McArdle, did some work evaluating a project that involved teenagers on the autistic spectrum using horses for therapy. Many of the participants found communicating with a stranger difficult. Karen met the teenagers informally with the horses, and interviews, in the form of informal chats, were held in the presence of a trusted therapist to help the young people to feel more comfortable. In some cases, two teenagers were interviewed together for companionship. Although the participants had limited speech, they used strong sounds and gestures to express their delight and some of their learning at being with the horses.

Voice is also important for the pragmatic reason that it is often the most colourful and telling evidence we can supply, and enables people to be frank and authentic in communicating their experience of a project or service. Our experience is that councillors find it more telling to hear the voice of one participant than be presented with a handful of reports.

One example from our experiences as practitioners is that of a community worker at an academic conference who wanted to tell the story of a successful project involving people with learning disabilities. She sought permission to stage a theatrical performance about the confidence and learning that had taken place and it was a resounding success. The participants with learning disabilities rose to the occasion and enjoyed the limelight immensely, demonstrating their growth in confidence and the things they had learned about themselves through small sketches. Writing and speaking in public gives power over others, in terms of being able to influence the lives and ideas of others.

> Power, status, values and attitudes towards writers and writing are all closely interconnected with each other, and with the questions of who writes about what and for whom, why this matters and why it is like this. (Clark and Ivanič, 1997, p 36)

Why present evidence?

So far, we have focused on the presentation of findings to funders, decision makers and participants. We find it helpful to think of presentation in terms of the '3Ps' – policy, professional, personal. You can influence policy through your presentations to government and funders. This is important, as it is often difficult to communicate the importance of work in the community because of its complexity. You may also influence the policy of your own organisation, which may remain the same or change to accommodate new knowledge in the light of your findings. The professional dimension of presentation is also important, as it enables you to contribute to the professional knowledge of other professionals, who will learn from your experience. Finally, presentation enables you to learn personally about the effectiveness of what you do; it will provide affirmation of what you do, hopefully, and areas for development or change.

How to present evidence?

There are no hard-and-fast rules about how evidence is presented (Robson, 2017), but, as outlined earlier, you need to think of the expectations of the audience. If you have made a firm evaluation, to do it justice you should probably produce a more formal report. If, however, your evidence is about winning a prize for effectiveness, publicity in newsletters or the press would be more appropriate. We have already suggested that you think creatively about presentation of evidence of impact. Inviting decision makers to visit a project or service is a good and positive way of communicating its ethos. Press coverage contributes to the impact of other forms of evidence. Blogs, ezines and social media are all possibilities for showing the impact of what you do.

Celebration and competitions

When thinking about presenting evidence, entering a competition is probably not the first thing that would spring to mind. However, this can be a really valuable way of validating the impact of your work in the eyes of funders, decision makers, the wider public and, most importantly, to the participants themselves. Many national organisations invite bids for evidence of effective and impactful work and then hold a celebratory event for the successful projects. Such events are often publicised in the local press, on websites, on YouTube or even on television. They can be a very powerful affirmation of learner achievements and help participants to reflect on the journey they have taken. Success often breeds success and participants often want to encourage other people to take part in their experiences and sometimes end up taking on the role of tutor themselves.

One of the recipients of a national award sums up his thoughts as follows:

> 'Well, we're very honoured to get the award. We always thought we had a good project but to be recognised by a national body – yeah – it makes us feel good and it probably helps us demonstrate that we're probably on the right path.'

Choosing what to say

The how of what to write or speak about also includes the need to be balanced and positive in what you say. Be aware, if you work for the government, of the political impact of what is said. This does not mean suppressing thoughts, just being aware of the impact on you, your work and your participants. Perhaps it goes without saying that you should be truthful, but this includes not exaggerating the impact of what has been done.

Choice is important in thinking about what to present (McArdle, 2018). We highlight some aspects of what we have found out and neglect others. Zimmermann (2015) discusses how every choice involves values and it is important to be aware of this. McArdle (2018) describes how objective knowledge is not possible in either quantitative or qualitative evidence. Even when we use numbers, we are making choices; our personal intuition and prior knowledge will influence what we notice.

> Knowledge is thus always the action of integrating particulars into a coherent whole. And this integration does not happen all by itself but requires personal engagement. As in any key areas of human knowledge this integrative work depends on the training, personal convictions and imaginative power of the scientist. (Zimmerman, 2015, p 123)

If you substitute the word 'practitioner' for 'scientist' in this quotation, you will see how who we are affects what we interpret evidence to mean and, therefore, how we present such evidence to others. Being conscious of this helps us to be clear about what we wish to present to others that is justified by our evidence. The 'spirit' of the evidence can be assured if we refer back to what participants have said, so quotations are important but cannot form the whole report. We need to make the link for the reader with the quality of what has been done in a project.

Often work is presented in a spoken format and this can be daunting to the practitioner, who may be fearful of difficult questions or critique. Confidence does come with practice. There are a few key principles to keep in mind:

• ensure you know what you want to say;
• think about the (up to) three main points you wish to make;
• plan your presentation as a story with scene setting, main action and an ending;
• plan, write and try to remember what you want to say;
• have bullet point notes to hand;
• practise timing – you must keep to the time or you will annoy the audience;
• practise with a sympathetic colleague who will provide helpful feedback;
• keep media to a minimum if you are nervous.

Communications strategies can be used to deal with difficult questions or comments. Acknowledging politely comments you cannot deal with, and moving on, is one strategy. You can also throw difficult questions back to the audience for a point of view. If asked about something you have not thought of, you may want to thank the questioner, ask for their opinion or say you will go away and give it attention. If you do not know the answer, you can simply say so, bearing in mind that you are the expert and know more about this than anyone else.

Self as author

As we are asking you to be creative in your presentation, it may be helpful when thinking about your writing to consider yourself and your impact on readers. In a seminal work on writing and identity, Roz Ivanič (1998) discusses the identity of the author. She is writing about the academic context, but the principles apply to practitioners. She states that there are three ways of thinking about identity as an author:

- the autobiographical self;
- the discoursal self;
- the self as author.

The autobiographical self is the identity the author brings as a result of their social history. For example, writing about residential care as a social worker may be influenced by the social worker having been fostered as a child. The discoursal self is related to the values, beliefs and power relations in the social context and how these are consciously or unconsciously conveyed in the text. The social worker, for example, may have picked up that children in residential care have a poor reputation and may choose to counter this consciously. The self as author is how you choose to present yourself in the text in terms of the writer's voice and position. The social worker may choose to write as an authority on children in the care system or 'looked after children', or may choose to write from her autobiographical perspective with insights from her experience.

Ethics

Ethical judgements are important in presenting data. At the very least you need to be sure that no person is identified in a report or presentation without their informed consent. This is often overlooked in the case of films or videos, so be sure to get everyone's consent before showing media such as these. You should also ensure that people are not recognisable in reports from details about their circumstances unless they are happy with this.

You should also think about the impact of what you intend to say on participants or the wider community. To suggest that a community lacks community spirit, for example, will demotivate the few people who do volunteer. This is where being balanced has an ethical dimension. To describe poverty in a suburb and to refer to its troubled population runs the risk of stereotyping residents. You can be truthful about deprivation, while being careful about the dignity of those you are describing. Recognising contributions is important, by acknowledging all stakeholders and partners, and indeed participants, albeit not necessarily by name in the latter case. If there is joint authorship, make sure the presentation is attributed to all contributors. Finally, you should avoid plagiarism, and ensure that you acknowledge all other sources of information or data used. Referencing can be daunting, but is essentially a matter of including the name of the author, the title of the publication, the date it was published and the publisher and place of publication (found usually inside the front cover) in the same format.

Visual presentation

Pictures do indeed tell a thousand words, and it is important to make presentations strong and attractive visually, whether by providing graphics in a PowerPoint presentation or producing a finished film. The eye is a primary sense and, as such, a primary sense for acquiring information. We consider that the eye communicates at a number of levels other than the conscious level. We have an emotional response, usually to pictures and often at a sub-conscious level that becomes conscious on reflection. Pictures capture an incident in a moment; there is a distillation of time. We are highly interpretative of what we see and a picture will be interpreted at a number of levels by each individual who sees it. Moving images, we suggest, are viewed in a quasi-dream state. We are not watching as we do in real life; rather we are seeing moving images while we are stationary. Combined with sound in a film, this is a very stimulating medium and provokes emotions and reflection.

Using theatre is a very strong and powerful visual and audible means of presenting evidence of impact. It is not necessarily 'real', but invokes thoughts and reflections on real experiences and aspects of our communities and lives. It is usually a very enjoyable experience for participants, who, rather than exposing themselves in a given situation, can choose to represent someone similar to them, so it can be a safe form of expression for some. Such visual media offer the audience an opportunity to praise and appreciate the evidence. When we use pictures or film, we are selecting, making judgements about a distilled moment or moments that we want to communicate. We are in effect making an argument in pictorial form. We can show context or main event; we can show reality and an insider view.

There is a powerful control element in what we choose to disclose in a film or picture. Images, unlike reality, can be viewed multiple times and can be a source of reflection. Picture and films are very strong in showing 'voice'; they provide visibility for those who may be seldom heard and seen. They are an authentic way of showing evidence of change, as it is the participants rather than the writer of a report who describe any change that has occurred. Pictures and films reinforce evidence of behavior, showing enjoyment, for example, or participation. They capture moments in time that the audience can then evaluate.

The downside of using pictures and films is that individuals may be identifiable and targeted through their visibility. It is crucial ethically to get informed consent from all participants and allow them to agree on the audience. It is important not to lose control of the images, for example by using them in social media without the agreement of participants. Another downside of visual images is that they are an interpretation of reality, and can be used to create something that is not real but looks real. This may be justifiable, but should be considered ethically – is it in the best interests of participants and, importantly, is it truthful?

Using visual images stimulates self-reflection on the part of the participant. This can be a positive experience, but may also make participants self-conscious and worried, and lead to fears of being rejected by the viewer. Practitioners should handle such situations carefully and sympathetically, for example, by showing positive behaviours so that the individual is not reinforced in negative behaviours or identity, and contextualising images so that viewers do not draw the wrong conclusions. It is important to think carefully about who has control over the picture content; it can be an empowering and authentic tool, and is essentially a creative process that can engage participants well.

In discussing the use of images for impact, we assume that you have already engaged with the participants. It is crucial that the images are acceptable to the people or contexts in them, and the participants do not feel 'used' or experience any of the negative emotions mentioned previously. We must also be conscious of the impact of showing a negative picture of a community on its residents' reputation and identity. Apart from a fundamental ability to engage with participants, the skills required to obtain images can be highly sophisticated or quite simple. Most of us have a mobile phone or camera and are well able to help others take 'selfies'. Many of us will also have access to video cameras and people with editing skills.

Distribution of knowledge

Once you have prepared a report or have given a talk about a project or service, it is important to think about distributing the information through your networks rather than leaving reports to gather dust on shelves. If you do a theatre presentation, inform the newspapers and other media. Think about your stakeholders – policy makers, professionals and participants. How will each group get to hear about your work? It may be as simple as putting an item on a meeting agenda. You should also consider the best time for your presentation. It may be at a crucial juncture in the project as well as at the end. It is an important part of your planning, discussed further in the next chapter.

Challenge questions

1. How integral to your work is gathering evidence?
2. How could you integrate research and evaluation into your practice to form the basis of evidence?
3. What are three facets of your identity as an author/presenter?
4. How could you present and celebrate success with your participants?
5. What creative skills could you bring to bear on presentations?

References

Brinkmann, S. and Kvale, S. (2015) *Interviews: Learning the Craft of Qualitative Research Interviewing*, Thousand Oaks, CA: Sage.

Clark, R. and Ivanič, R. (1997) *The Politics of Writing*, Abingdon: Routledge.

Education Scotland (2016) *How Good is the Learning and Development in our Community?: Evaluation Resource*, Livingston: Education Scotland.

Ivanič, R. (1998) *Writing and Identity*, Amsterdam: John Benjamins.

Miller, E., Donoghue, G. and Holland-Batt, S. (2015) 'You could scream the place down' five poems on the experience of aged care, *Qualitative Inquiry*, *21*(5): 410-17.

McArdle, K. (2018) *Freedom Research in Education: Becoming an Autonomous Researcher*, Cham: Palgrave Macmillan.

Potter, J. (2004) *Representing Reality: Discourse, Rhetoric and Social Construction*, London: Sage.

Robson, C. (2017) *Small-Scale Evaluation: Principles and Practice* (2nd edn), London: Sage.

Scottish Government (2007) *LEAP: A Manual for Learning Evaluation and Planning in Community Learning and Development*, Edinburgh: Scottish Government, available at https://www2.gov.scot/Publications/2007/12/05101807/2 (accessed 6 March 2019).

Zimmermann, J. (2015) *Hermeneutics: A Very Short Introduction*, Oxford: Oxford University Press.

5

Planning and evaluating

Karen McArdle, Kirsty Forrester and Ed Garrett

Introduction

This book is not simply about evaluation. It is much broader than this, as we have already described in Part I. It is primarily about gathering evidence of impact, but you are very likely to encounter evaluation; to want to undertake evaluation; and to learn from what you find out. Chapter 15, on self-evaluation, will contribute to this and should be read in conjunction with this chapter. Evaluation, like presentation of findings, should be a part of your planning process. This chapter considers planning in an evaluation context and also considers mixed methods of gathering data or evidence. It tackles a particularly common form of evaluation, which is the cost–benefit analysis of a project or service, and considers the benefits of radical research, a slight change from the usual approaches to evaluation.

Evaluation

Evaluation research or evaluation is a distinctive type of formal research, so is at the far right-hand side of the evidence continuum (see Figure 1.1). There are many competing definitions and understandings of evaluation. Terminology is used very loosely. Sometimes it is used as a noun, so a questionnaire is termed an evaluation. This, we propose, is an incorrect use of the term. Stuart and colleagues (2015) describe evaluation as a specific form of research that ascertains the number, amount, value, quality or importance of programmes. These features are also clearly embedded in our concept of impact. The primary purpose of evaluation is not to acquire new knowledge but to study the effectiveness with which existing knowledge is used to guide practical action (Clarke, 1999) and this is the definition we choose to use. Formal evaluation involves engaging with all stakeholders in a project. It is frequently externally conducted, although the degree of formality may vary. Any evaluation you conduct will be framed as research, which means having research questions that describe what you want to find out; having a relevant and appropriate methodology, including sample; applying ethical standards; ensuring validity; and analysing and interpreting your findings. This is not a book about how to do research, but you will find all the aforementioned elements covered in the different chapters in this section of the book.

Planning

When planning a project or service, it is critical that evaluation is built into the planning process. Evaluation is how you know you were successful in doing what you intended to do, and will identify any other useful outcomes too. It is important before we discuss planning to distinguish between outputs and outcomes, as both are routinely described in evaluation. Outputs are what we have planned to do and actually do; and outcomes are the wider impacts of what we do. So, an output might be an adult learning programme in the health field and the outcome might be improved health and wellbeing in the community. Inputs are the resources used to execute a policy, programme or project and include money, staffing, volunteers and other resources.

There is an analytical phase to planning during which you examine the contextual circumstances, including both characteristics and any anticipated changes. You will probably assess demand or need and you will consider the characteristics of your population. The second phase is design, during which you will look at options, having regard to constraints and opportunities. The third phase involves looking at the feasibility of the project you have chosen and, accordingly, evaluation of exactly what you will do both during and at the end of the project. The final phase involves devising the timescale and a development brief, funding proposal or set of clear plans with costs.

Planning is typically framed not as a linear but as a cyclical process, where a need is identified and the planner decides what to do or what needs to change. This gives rise to the question of how we know change has taken place, which leads to a reassessment of needs. So planning is about a cycle. Stuart and colleagues (2015) describe the reflective evaluative cycle. This is derived from Kolb's experiential learning cycle (1984), which may already be known to readers, and Lewin's action research model (1946). There are many models of cycles of evaluation but one simple method commonly used in Scotland in community work, for example, is the Learning Evaluation and Planning (LEAP) framework (Scottish Government, 2007), see Figure 5.1, previously mentioned in Chapter 4.

LEAP is driven by the following questions:

- What is the need in the community?
- What difference do we want to make?

Figure 5.1: LEAP process

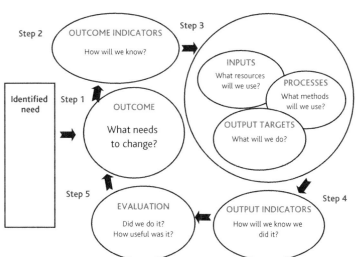

Source: derived from Scottish Government, 2007

- How do we know whether we made a difference?
- How shall we go about making the difference?
  - What resources shall we use?
  - What methods shall we use?
  - How shall we use them?
- How are we making sure it is happening?
- Have we made a difference?
- What are the lessons we have learned?
- What should we do now?

This model allows us to:

- focus our work clearly;
- ensure that our work is purposeful and relevant to participants;
- work with other stakeholders;
- develop action plans that match resources, methods and actions to our purposes;
- monitor the implementation of our plans;
- learn what works and what does not;
- address issues of inclusion and targeting by identifying clearly who benefits from our work;
- build evidence collection into our ongoing practice; and
- build a body of evidence on which we can draw for the purpose of self-evaluation at individual, team, agency or partnership levels (derived from Scottish Government, 2007).

It is quite clear that evaluation must be built into the planning and may be driven by the key questions outlined in Figure 5.1. It is also quite clear that evaluation is embedded in the processes of a project and, accordingly, project plans should accommodate evaluation and the achievement of key performance indicators (KPIs). A KPI is simply a measure of progress towards outcomes. So if a project plans, over three years, to enrol 150 participants, a KPI might be that, at the end of year one, 50 have been enrolled. One key and common approach to planning is undertake a SWOT analysis (of strengths, weaknesses, opportunities and threats) with stakeholders to see where this leads you in your planning. We suggest altering the sequence of SWOT, to avoid concluding the analysis with the negative associations of threats.

Radical and freedom research

We mentioned earlier that evaluation is a form of research, so it is important to think about the 'kind of research' we choose to do for evaluative purposes. The term 'radical research' is described by Schostak and Schostak (2008) as a question of values, among other things. They describe the purpose of radical research as being an alternative to methods that perpetuate inequality and disadvantage.

> It is an approach that maintains a radical openness to difference while seeking to build communities of support for difference…. It is about engaging with change. Research like any other social practice can become routinised and compromised by the powerful. (Schostak and Schostak, 2008, p 8)

The authors further argue that radical research is essential to the promotion of creative, supportive relations between individuals and the communities they compose, which is important for all the social professions. Value judgements are made at every stage of the research process, so we must always conscious of what we are doing from a values perspective (McArdle, 2018), as this will affect the people with whom we work and who we involve in our evaluation research. McArdle (2018) argues that we should always challenge orthodoxy in research; research is socially constructed and enshrines power dimensions. She refers to research that challenges orthodoxy as 'freedom research'. How we frame the research we do will be governed by how we view the world, whether we consider that others should be in harmony with the dominant discourses of society, or whether there is space for diversity, difference and, indeed, conflict.

Schostak and Schostak (2008) claim that evaluation can either be framed according to the God's-eye view of how the world should be, or the multiple views of people at street level. McArdle (2018) proposes that in our evaluations we should question the assumptions behind the judgements we make about how the world should be. If we run employability programmes, we are making an implicit value judgement that employment is indeed 'right' for all people and should therefore be encouraged. This begs the question of the value we place on volunteering or being unemployed and in receipt of benefits. If we are evaluating an employability programme, should we just 'count' or place value on employment gained or should we look more broadly than this at individual growth and development in our evaluation?

Denzin and Giardina (2010) argue for an ethical stance in the research we do.

> Acting towards others as we wish others to treat us is clear, unarguable, and the intuitive way to live harmoniously in the human world. It proceeds from an understanding of human dignity – we regard other basically like ourselves. Its secret is avoiding a list of prohibited acts and providing a way to think about the common good. (p 52)

As we are dealing in evaluation with the ideas and practice of ourselves or others, we need to think about the vulnerabilities of the people associated with the projects we evaluate. Research can be conducted in a way that recognises human rights and vulnerabilities. It is most important in evaluation not to fall into the trap of a morally and politically neutral stance for research where this is damaging to the stakeholders. Social processes are saturated with rights, negotiation of rights and, alas, violations of rights (Denzin and Giardina, 2010). Evaluation should involve considering questions about the political ownership of the project. How the project was implemented from the outset? What is the origin of the idea of the project? Who decided there was a need for the project? Who made the choices about the project and how?

The following quotation from Clarke (1999) shows how evaluation differs from other forms of social research and emphasises some of the sensitivities that demand negotiation skills

> Evaluation is primarily concerned with determining the merit, worth or value of an established policy or intervention. This makes it a unique form of social inquiry. Emphasis is placed on providing practical knowledge to aid decision making processes; a

feature that has led to evaluation being seen as a type of policy research. By virtue of its practical orientation and policy focus, evaluation not only has political effects, but is also influenced by political forces. This has implications for the nature of the relationship between the researcher and researched. In an evaluation study there will be numerous individuals and groups who have vested interests in the programme under review ... evaluators must negotiate whose questions will be addressed and whose interests will be served. (p 3)

Being participatory is important to respecting the rights of stakeholders, including participants. It has an intrinsically critical edge (Denzin and Giardina, 2010). It requires that people collaborate on a more equal footing than in the traditional relationship between the researcher and the researched. Involving stakeholders is crucial to evaluation. This needs to be done authentically or we risk the accusation of pseudo-empowerment where the powerful appease the less powerful by giving the appearance of consultation, without allowing their views to change the project itself.

Types of evaluation

Exactly who does the evaluation is a matter for decision making. Clarke (1999) provides a helpful summary of the advantages and disadvantages of using internal or external evaluators. It is important, whatever your final choice, to try to overcome the disadvantages.

Box 5.1 Using internal or external evaluators

Advantages

Internal evaluators will be:

• familiar with the history, background, policies, issues and culture of the organisation;

- likely to be more committed to implementing evaluation recommendations, having been responsible for producing them;
- likely to know the participants and key stakeholders well.

External evaluators have:

- an independent stance and offer a fresh perspective;
- an overview of other organisations for comparative purposes;
- a knowledge and experience of research methods;
- a resilience to management persuasion;
- greater credibility because of independence.

Disadvantages

Internal evaluators may:

- have a vested interest in an outcome;
- be over-influenced by history and organisational issues;
- be over-influenced by management.

External evaluators may be:

- expensive;
- ignorant of internal matters, meaning their judgements may not reflect complex reality;
- influenced by need to secure future contracts;
- insensitive to organisational norms and relationships.

(Derived in part from Clarke, 1999, p 23)

Stakeholders

In evaluation, it is important to make sure that everyone who needs to be consulted is consulted, not just participants, albeit the latter are, of course, important. This means including all partners, managers and staff, and anyone else who may have a vested interest in the project. If you do not include all stakeholders, we suggest that you are not conducting an evaluation; you are more likely to be gathering evidence of impact, which is equally valid, but is a more restricted process that needs to work cumulatively.

Critical reflection and self-evaluation

Critical reflection and self-evaluation are discussed in Chapters 3 and 15, respectively. Here we wish to signal the importance of these to evaluative processes. In evaluation, we inevitably make judgements and it is important that these are both honest and authentic, as well as being critical. Evaluation is not useful if it is all positive; improvement is always possible, and this demands that project staff are comfortable and able to use feedback. This does not mean it needs to be a negative experience; rather, it is about growth, development and learning.

Judgement

It is not possible to think of evaluation without thinking of making sound judgements about the data we generate. It is not the role of this text to explain data analysis, as this would take a whole book in itself. Instead, we simply need to know that we will generate data and need to make sense of it. The best forms of analysis combine looking at what is said (or drawn or performed) and how it was said. You must examine critically what you have found out and apply it to the context of the evaluation. It is important here to stress that you should always look for the obverse of what is suggested by the data or first comes to mind. So, if you find that a lot of participants did not like a service, you would look for those who did to provide balance. The same applies if most people did like a service, you should look for the minority who did not to see why this might be the case and to look for areas for improvement.

It is important here to discuss sensitivity. It is important to present criticism in a way that is developmental and not negative. If you present negative findings in a negative way, this is likely to cause a negative reaction and is likely to be challenged or ignored, neither of which is helpful. Think instead about the learning that can be derived from the finding and express it in this way. Always put yourself in the shoes of the people/stakeholders who will read or hear the evaluation and think how they will react.

Formative and summative evaluation

Evaluation can be formative or summative. Formative evaluation is a method of undertaking evaluation during a project to track its progress towards stated goals, and is intended to provide information for improvement. Summative evaluation is judging the worth of a programme at the end of its activities. Both are very useful and can be blended when reporting findings of an evaluation.

Mixed methods

All of the methods of gathering evidence included in this book can be used for evaluation. Focus groups, interviews, observation and questionnaires are all appropriate means of generating data. McArdle (2018) argues that any method is acceptable as long as ethical implications are handled sensitively. We do not intend to discuss particular methods in this chapter; rather, we consider mixed methods, which we consider are most frequently appropriate, though by no means always, for generating triangulated data.

Denzin (1970) identifies four types of triangulation: data, investigator, theoretical and methodological triangulation (triangulation in this context means using more than one concept to come closer to the truth than could be achieved by using a single concept). Data triangulation means that data are collected in multiple contexts or at different times; investigator triangulation means involving more than one researcher; theoretical triangulation involves using multiple theories to look at the data; and methodological triangulation involves triangulation between methods. All of these triangulations are of benefit to an evaluation.

Chelimsky (1985) describes three kinds of question that are commonly asked during evaluation. These are descriptive questions, which ask how many people take part in a project and what form participation takes; normative questions, which ask how the project is meeting its stated outcomes and outputs; and cause-and-effect questions, which ask whether or not a project has worked and whether it is likely to work in the future. Evaluation involves measuring costs and outputs/outcomes; asking whether a project has been carried out as intended; seeking the reactions and responses of participants; and questioning whether the project has met perceived needs.

Mixed methods are sometimes referred to as the 'third path' of research orientations, but it is arguably better to refer to mixed methodologists as the third research community, as they represent an alternative to the dichotomy of qualitative and quantitative research preferences. They work primarily in a pragmatist paradigm and are interested in both narrative and numerical data (Teddlie and Tashakkori, 2009). Mixed methods research has emerged as an orientation only during the past 30 years. Mixed methodologists advocate using whatever methodological tools are required to answer the questions posed. The research design embraces both qualitative and quantitative approaches, integrating findings in a single evaluation. A research methodology is a broad approach to scientific inquiry, specifying how research questions should be asked and answered (Teddlie and Tashakkori, 2009).

We now pause for a moment to focus on induction and deduction. Induction is where theories or ideas are derived from with*in* the data. Deduction where the theories are *de*duced prior to data collection and are explored in the research. Inductive ideas come after the event and deductive ideas come before the event, as hypotheses to be tested. Deduction is used in quantitative studies, induction in qualitative studies. Mixed methods use both; deductive and inductive logic are integrated in analysis. What this means is that your evaluation will include theories or ideas that you will test in the quantitative part of the study (for example, a survey using a questionnaire), and that you will derive theories or ideas from the qualitative part of your study (for example, interviews or focus groups). You must then balance these or synthesise the ideas so that together they illuminate the research questions used for your evaluation. You will look for similarities and differences in the data from both sets, asking the question of whether the two sets of data confirm one idea. The following case study provides an example.

A researcher in Western Australia wished to evaluate the provision of a network of rural youth clubs. She designed a questionnaire and sent it out to the clubs. The main finding was that there was a general rather bland dissatisfaction with living in a rural community. The research design involved qualitative interviews with a small number of the 300 participants who had returned questionnaires. These found that the reason for the dissatisfaction was that young men predominated in the clubs in order to meet young women, and that failure to fulfil this deep need led to depression and fear of the absence of family life in the future. The two datasets were brought together to show this conclusion.

There is a range of factors you might explore in evaluation. We have already discussed outcomes, whether what has been achieved was what was intended. This range of factors might include, among other things, distance travelled. This means that people are measured against the outcomes of the project at the beginning and at the end to see how far they have come (Stuart et al, 2105). Process evaluation measures what is happening during the course of a programme. Theory evaluation means testing a theory about why a programme works (Robson, 2017). You might also wish to measure the quality of a project, which must be determined according to criteria, and may involve a high standard of outcome, for example, or a high rating by participants.

Cost–benefit analysis

Cost–benefit analysis (CBA) is simply a method of planning and evaluating the economic impacts of projects. The term 'benefits' should alert us to the fact that value judgements are being made about the benefits of a project and the legitimacy of the costs involved. Implicit in these decisions are some judgements about efficiency, so the value of the outputs/ outcomes is greater than the cost of the inputs. Costing social outcomes is considered in Chapter 11. Also implicit is some objective of optimising or seeking the 'best' state of affairs for a project, where the optimal cost results in the best attainable outcome. Once again, implicit in CBA is a consideration of direct costs and direct benefits. Undertaking a CBA involves measuring the physical and human resources invested in a project and balancing these as a ratio to the benefits produced. This can be expressed numerically as a ratio between, for example, the cost per head of a project and the value of the benefit. So, for example in the UK this could be expressed as £50: £350, where the cost of a training course on housing policy is £50 per participant, and the benefit in terms of the saving in staff time for remediation of a situation is £350 per participant. In the case of 20 participants, this could be expressed as £1,000: £7,000 or 1:7. The following case study is an example of one of us, Karen McArdle, conducting a CBA.

> Karen did a CBA for a project that signposted participants to community resources to assist with mental health and wellbeing, rather than those individuals attending overstretched general practitioner services, typically for around four visits. She did a literature search to find the typical cost of a GP appointment and multiplied this by four. She also found the cost of a single intervention with signposting (participants typically only needed one intervention), taking into account all costs and overheads. The result was a CBA ratio of cost to the taxpayer expressed as cost of signposting intervention: cost of GP intervention. The result was that the signposting was considerably better value.
>
> The most important aspects of the CBA were:
>
> • measuring like with like;
> • ensuring that the figures were absolutely rock solid;
> • including details of the calculations and parameters used when reporting the findings of the CBA.

On-the-spot evidence gathering

When conducting a broad evaluation, it is important to use methods that are creative, innovative and attractive to overcome consultation fatigue and to engage people successfully; moreover, it is simply a thoughtful thing to do. Using drawings and post-it notes is an easy way to do this. If you have the resources, using theatre or other arts can be very informative.

For narrower evaluations, for example, for training sessions or workshops, on-the-spot evidence gathering is a useful tool. A questionnaire is not an evaluation, as stated earlier in this chapter, and we hope to wean community workers away from using them inappropriately. We suggest that questionnaires are often used simply because they are straightforward, non-threatening, appear to be 'academic' and are unlikely to elicit unbiased feedback, and so are relatively safe. An alternative approach might be to give participants questions to answer and leave the room. They could then discuss the questions among themselves and nominate a spokesperson to provide feedback after ten to 15 minutes, when you are called back in. Such feedback is likely to be unbiased and considered; it represents consensus and obviates the necessity of putting individuals on the spot. It demands on the part of the trainer or facilitator a willingness to hear the truth about what has worked and what has not worked as framed by the participants, rather than a positive whitewash about the food, the comfort of the room and the performance of the facilitator derived from a questionnaire.

Box 5.2 provides an example of the kind of tool you might use in evaluating practice. It is derived from a tool used by Aberdeenshire Council, which covers a largely rural and expansive area of Scotland. It is not sufficient for a full evaluation, as it does not involve undertaking the relevant research, but it is a way of judging and monitoring progress towards outcomes and outputs, and provides a useful summary of evaluating practice.

Box 5.2 Illuminating practice in lifelong learning and leisure

• Project/work title: Safe drive – manage the road

Summary

In 2012, a four-week pilot course on safe driving was delivered in the Milltown area. This was delivered as partnership project and was targeted at 16–18-year-olds. It ran in the evenings in the grounds of Milltown Secondary School. In conjunction, a drama presentation capturing key safety messages was created with the involvement of participants and delivered to an audience of fourth-year pupils (age 15–16) as part of an early intervention approach.

What was the need to be addressed and how did you know?

In the past year, road accidents between 17 and 25 year olds in the Milltown area had increased by 20%. Police data identified this worrying trend. The issue was highlighted at a multi-agency planning meeting as a priority concern. A partnership action plan was put in place.

Who was involved?

• Police Scotland local team;
• local private driving school;
• Milltown Secondary School guidance staff;
• community learning and development (CLD) staff;
• arts development staff;
• local Young Farmers' groups.

What resources were needed?

• Funding from the Community Safety programme;
• school venue;
• staff from Police Scotland, Milltown Secondary School, CLD, the arts team;
• driving instructor time;

- promotional material;
- volunteer time from the Young Farmers' groups.

What actually happened?

- Four free sessions were held on a Thursday evening from 6.30pm to 9pm.
- Guidance staff in the secondary school promoted participation and coordinated a drama presentation for fourth-years.
- Police Scotland and the local driving school worked together to create the core programme and delivered elements including safe on-the-road driving experiences in adapted vehicles.
- CLD staff targeted young people not in school and enabled certain individuals to attend the course.
- Arts development staff worked with participants to frame a 10-minute presentation that was delivered in school to all fourth-years as an early intervention programme.

What was the output of the project?

- A training course was designed and piloted with 17 participants.
- A drama presentation was created and delivered to 87 peers.
- Materials highlighting road safety issues were designed.

What impact did the work have?

- Strengthened local partnership working.
- Eighty-five per cent of those who signed up completed the course.
- In the past six months there has been a 10% reduction in road accidents.
- The programme has been adopted by two neighbouring local authorities.
- The programme has been approved and used in three other secondary schools.
- Young Farmers' groups have had requests to repeat the programme from farmers and agricultural companies who employ high levels of young workers.

How do you know?

- Feedback from participants – using video diary;
- statistics from Police Scotland;

• evaluations from drama presentation;
• minutes of follow-up meeting.

What were the lessons learned?

Of the 17 participants only two were females, yet the statistics tell us that females are equally likely to be involved in road accidents in this age group. More targeting of female participants should be a feature of future programmes. The timing worked well – early evening. More time spent on the driving activities would be an improvement. The budgeting was on target.

Reporting methods for evaluations are covered in Chapter 4.

Acting on recommendations

We have already discussed the importance of critical reflection, and the purpose of evaluation is not just to show how things have worked, but also to identify areas for improvement, which always exist. It is crucial that stakeholders act on evaluation findings, otherwise the exercise has been a waste of time and effort. Reasons for a lack of implementation include failure to buy into the evaluation process, so that a report sits on a shelf and is ignored; unwillingness on the part of managers to implement recommendations; and defensiveness and unpreparedness for professional or personal growth on the part of staff, leading to recommendations being ignored or argued away.

These problems can be avoided by negotiating and engaging managers and staff early on in the evaluation process so that they have a sense of ownership of the findings. Staff can be supported in learning techniques for avoiding defensiveness through critical reflection on the findings in an environment free from blame.

Evaluation reports should always be balanced with positive findings and areas for improvement, both of which always exist. It is also important that all those who have been involved in the evaluation receive feedback on their input. All stakeholders should receive copies of the full report and participants of the project should either receive the full report or a summary of the key findings. This is important because they have given their time and consideration to the evaluation.

Challenge questions

1. How did you plan your project/service? Was evaluation built in or left to the end?
2. What are your main hopes and fears about evaluating your project?
3. Who are your key stakeholders? How do you involve them in your project improvement?
4. What do you think are the main strengths and limitations of your project?

References

Chelimsky, E. (1985) Comparing and contrasting auditing and evaluation: some notes on their relationship, *Evaluation Review*, 9(4): 483–503.

Clarke, A. (1999) *Evaluation Research: An introduction to Principles, Methods and Practice*, London: Sage.

Denzin, N.K. (1970) *The Research Act in Sociology*, London: Butterworths.

Denzin, N.K. and Giardina, M.D. (2010) *Qualitative Inquiry and Human Rights*, Walnut Creek, CA: Left Coast Press.

McArdle, K. (2018) *Freedom Research in Education: Becoming an Autonomous Researcher*, Cham: Palgrave Macmillan.

Robson, C. (2017) *Small-Scale Evaluation: Principles and Practice*, London: Sage.

Schostak, J. and Schostak, J. (2008) *Radical Research: Designing, Developing and Writing Research to make a Difference*, Abingdon: Routledge.

Scottish Government (2007) *LEAP: A Manual for Learning Evaluation and Planning in Community Learning and Development*, Edinburgh: Scottish Government, available at https://www2. gov.scot/Publications/2007/12/05101807/2 (accessed 6 March 2019).

Stuart, K., Maynard, L. and Rouncefield, C. (2015) *Evaluation Practice for Projects with Young People: A Guide to Creative Research*, London: Sage.

Teddlie, C. and Tashakkori, A. (2009) *Foundations of Mixed Methods Research: Integrating Quantitative and Qualitative Approaches in the Social and Behavioral Sciences*, London: Sage.

6

Anecdote and observation

Ed Garrett and Karen McArdle

Introduction

This chapter looks at the importance of anecdote and observation. As practitioners, we constantly observe, as a matter of course, the groups, communities and individuals with whom we work. For example, when delivering training to a group, Ed looks for signs that show him if the training is going well or not; how people respond to tasks; how engaged participants are; and how they relate to each other. We use these observations, sometimes explicitly but often implicitly, to build our evidence of impact. So, a good understanding of the use of observation in showing evidence of impact is an invaluable skill for any practitioner, because it is something we all do anyway as part of our community work. Just as important, however, understanding exactly how we can use observation in building evidence is a key part of our practice as community workers and it can define our relationships with other professionals too. As Chapter 3 argued, as community workers, we often deal most closely with the local, the anecdotal and the historically situated, and this kind of knowledge is not always highly valued. Different forms of knowing are valued differently by different people. Observation is largely about this kind of local evidence, and if we can understand it better we can justify it better to others.

Different ways of observing

Observation, as a method, has a central place in social science research. This is not a book about research methods, but it is important to distinguish between different ways of observing to understand exactly what we do as practitioners working with communities. First, observation can be overt or covert. In covert observation, the observer participates in the community or group they are observing, without making this clear to that community or group. This approach can generally be ruled out as problematic ethically. As this book has stressed several times, the ethics of evidence gathering are as important as the actual evidence gathered. If communities are being observed as part of evidence gathering, they should be made aware of this. There may be some general observations we can make about communities that are valuable, but, as soon as we observe specific groups and individuals, we need to make our role clear (which it generally would be anyway, we suggest).

Observation needs to be overt, in that the community or group is aware of the observer in his/her role as observer. Overt observation has two main types: participant observation and non-participant observation.

In participant observation, the observer is acknowledged as an observer, but is also part of the community or involved in the community or group they are observing. An example of this would be a youth worker taking particular notes of the dynamics during an outdoor education activity.

In non-participant observation, the observer is again acknowledged as an observer, but observes the activities of a group or community, without taking part in them. One of us, Karen McArdle, did this kind of observation with children doing riding therapy, as described in Chapter 4. The young people were autistic and had no, or limited, spoken language, so she negotiated that she would be observing in sign language, then stood back to give them space and watched to check that they did not object to this.

Participant observation is a very valuable approach that can, in particular, provide rich understandings of groups and communities from the inside. It is the core of ethnographic research, used particularly in anthropology (Shah, 2017). Ethnographic research, however, requires skills, experience, time and a cultural commitment beyond what community practitioners can be expected to have. To be done properly, it also requires time and resources that are again beyond what most of us working with communities are able to afford. Nonetheless, there is still much to learn from participant observation, which can be a very useful means of gathering evidence of impact from the inside, and we shall return to it later.

Reasons for using non-participant observation

To help show how non-participant observation can be used and why it is useful, let us return to the example in Chapter 1 of Ryan and the groups he runs for people who have been recently bereaved. Ryan must provide funders with evidence of the effectiveness of these groups in helping people through the bereavement process. Initially, he decides to use a questionnaire as the best and most obvious way of gathering evidence. However, when the questionnaires have all been filled in and returned, the results are bland and do not quite fit with his sense of what the participants are getting from the group, based on his professional observation. In part, this may be a problem with the design of the questionnaire (covered in Chapter 7), but it also may be that his observations of the group necessarily provide a broader, deeper and more subtle scope than any questionnaire can have. It is not just that people may not respond entirely honestly to questionnaires, although clearly this does happen; lots of evidence suggests, for example, that people tend to significantly underreport their alcohol consumption compared with what might be observed (Zhao and Ji, 2014). It is also the case, we suggest, that observation allows for an openness and breadth of possible evidence that no questionnaire can achieve, as the questionnaire's veritable size will limit the amount of feedback a participant can choose to give.

The evidence gathered through observation is therefore very useful to Ryan, giving him a more complete understanding of the value of the group to the participants. Ryan observes changes in mood and behaviour. He has opportunities to see the nuances of the impact of his work. Non-participant observation is also useful because it involves the people who probably know best how the group is working for its members. It gives a genuine voice to the members of the group, unmediated by the demands of a questionnaire or a focus group, for example. It takes seriously the facilitator's observations of the group in action. Using observation is a recognition that our judgements as practitioners are important; we must have confidence in what our own observation tells us. We must also adopt a role of critical balance in observation, and ensure that we are seeing both good and bad rather than putting a rosy glow on our work. Objectivity is a very difficult frame of mind to achieve and we would argue that it may be impossible, given that we are not always aware of our own biases and implicit assumptions. It is important to aim for critical balance, however, as this assists with the credibility of what is observed.

Attribution

Observation is particularly useful, as the example of Ryan suggests, when the impact you are trying to achieve is quite complex and multifaceted. If you want to provide evidence that a job club has increased employability, you can look at people going on to get interviews and jobs, which requires little observation. If you wish to show evidence of increased confidence, as Ryan might want to with his groups, observing the relationships in the group will be extremely valuable. Observation can also be useful, in the same context, for showing evidence of attribution. It is often quite difficult to know exactly what outcome or output can be attributed to a project or intervention, compared with the effects of a wide range of other factors. Observation, because it can take into account the complexity of a situation, can be a reliable guide to attribution, if done with critical balance.

Challenges

The challenges to effective use of observation mostly involve making sure that we and others have confidence in ourselves as observers. Observation is unlikely to be the only way of evidencing impact (Iacono et al, 2009). Ryan, for example, probably uses questionnaires and interviews, as well as basic monitoring data such as attendance lists. Observations are part of the triangulation of evidence, the building-up of the picture. Confidence in observation is built and confirmed through these other sources of evidence and through critical balance.

Some observations may concern relatively uncontroversial facts, such as numbers of people at a group, or who spoke to whom, or even the words that people said. Confidence in such observations is best established by sensitive and solid ways of recording, and we come this later in this chapter. Other kinds of observation may appear more problematical, embodying the necessary partiality of the observer. This book has already made clear that we are all positioned in a social and cultural context and that this positionality affects how we observe the world around us (Lopez-Dicastillo and Belintxon, 2014). Take the example of working with an older people's group, in which all of the organisation is done by women with men simply coming along. The community worker may observe that the women feel put upon and the men feel excluded, and there may well be truth in these observations. However, these observations will be underpinned by the individual's understanding of equality and gender roles and will not necessarily be sensitive to the understandings and culture of a different generation.

Ensuring the robustness of our observations is a key part of developing professionalism. As discussed in Chapter 3, the process of reflexivity is an important way of reflecting on positionality and essentially asking the question, 'What is the self who is making these observations?' Accordingly, it is important to understand oneself as working with particular values in relation to equality and gender roles and that these values may not be understood in the same way by other people. We must also understand ourselves as actively constructing knowledge in relation to these values (Iacono et al, 2009), knowledge that may be taken at face value by our audience or contested. We all need to build opportunities for proper critical reflection into our work; this is a means to critical balance. Without this reflection, we, and others, may not be able to trust our observations.

There are other more practical challenges with the use of observation, in particular, that to be really effective, it can be quite time- and resource-intensive. This is not to say that it needs to involve the commitment of an anthropologist living with a community over a long period of time, but it does need enough time for trust and understanding to develop and provide a basis for meaningful observation. It is difficult for community workers to get much of a sense of change in a group from one or two visits. It will take time over many visits to build the relationships of trust that ensure people's interactions are authentic. As practitioners involved with communities and groups, you are already likely to work in this way, so it need not be extra work.

Finally, at the start of this chapter we noted that we almost inevitably observe all of the time during the course of our work. Sometimes we are aware of using these observations in showing evidence of impact. Often, we may not be so explicit, but these observations may influence our evidence anyway. We may interpret feedback from a questionnaire in the light of our observation of that group. If we make our observations as explicit as we can, we can subject them to the necessary process of reflexivity, reflection and discussion.

Recording observations

Good recording of observations is an important part of having confidence in them. Memory has a habit of recreating the past and should not be the only thing we rely on. As the philosopher Ludwig Wittgenstein said, in a different context, trying to confirm the truth of a memory by appealing to memory is like trying to confirm the accuracy of a newspaper article by looking at another copy of exactly the same newspaper. It confirms nothing (Wittgenstein, 1953). There are a range of ways of recording observations (Taylor-Powell and Steele, 1996). You may wish to use observation sheets, if you know what you are looking for at the outset. These are particularly useful if a number of different observers are involved, as they provide some consistency to the observations. Box 6.1 provides an example of an observation sheet that might be used across some training sessions, for example, although it could, of course, be adapted for a range of contexts:

Box 6.1 Sample observation sheet

Date
Session
Session leader
Participants

			Additional observations
Do participants respond positively to tasks?	Yes	No	
Do participants relate well to each other in problem solving activities?	Yes	No	
Do participants ask questions that show a developing understanding of the topic?	Yes	No	
Do the participants complete the tasks successfully?	Yes	No	

You could make sound or video recordings of discussions and group activities. These are more likely to be used by professional researchers, as it take times and skill to analyse them, but they are a good way of backing up your memories of an event. The method you are most likely to use to record observations is note taking. Anthropologists might call these field notes. The advantage of this method is the openness of the observation. There is no predetermined expectation of what you might observe. You just take notes at the time of what you have observed, or, if this is not possible, write up notes as soon as possible afterwards. Notes may take the form of a reflective diary that encourages thoughts on the nature of the observations, as well as reflections about yourself as the observer.

Whatever method you use to capture and record observations, it is important to get the basic facts: the time and date; the place; and any background information that is useful in understanding the observations.

Analysis of observations

It is important to make sense of observations, in order to make them a useful part of our evidence of impact. There is a danger of collecting lots of information and then not knowing what to do with it. Any quantitative data gathered through observation is fairly easy to collate and use. It is more difficult to makes sense of our notes or reflective diaries if they include lots of narrative observations. Anthropologists and other social researchers use sophisticated systems of coding (Zhao and Ji, 2014) to impose order on, and understand, their recorded observations. Again, as community work practitioners, we do not necessarily have the time or skills to do this. We can, however, learn from these researchers and look for patterns in our own observations. A reflective diary that may have already started to identify such patterns may be very useful for this, as well as discussion of the observational data with others.

Theory

It is worth reflecting a little on some of the theory behind observation in order to explore further why it might be so valuable to community practitioners and how we can best use it. Broadly speaking, philosophers argue that reality is either something that is independent of us and our thinking about it (realism) or that it is in some way actively created through our thinking and perceptions (idealism). Although this may seem abstract, it does matter for community workers, who are interested in how and why what we do works. In social science research, which is what we are involved with as community workers, these different philosophical traditions are represented by positivism and by phenomenology or interpretivism. For the positivist, the knowledge of reality is possible as something that exists independent of the researcher. For the phenomenologist or interpretivist, knowledge of reality is the creation of a dynamic and complex process that can never be independent of the researcher. So there is no objective reality out there that we can look into and know; it will always contain something of us.

Although, in practice, this distinction is much more nuanced than this brief summary can convey, observation sits clearly on one side of the divide. It is part of a phenomenological approach. Observation is, of course, a way of gathering information on facts and figures, rather in the positivist tradition, but its chief value lies in gathering what is missed by these facts and figures – namely, what is said and done (and not said and not done) by groups and individuals, all mediated through the observations and, it is hoped, reflections of the observer. For the observer, there is no reality without these people in it.

Understanding this distinction and observation's place in it is important for various reasons. In the course of our work in and with communities, we interact with people with different understandings of knowledge and the nature of evidence, and of how this evidence affects the way they see and value what we do. For example, the voluntary or third sector provides a vast range of services and activities in health and social care, from lunch clubs to peer support groups and befriending schemes. In our experience, doctors and other health professionals are sometimes reluctant to make referrals to such services and activities. In part, this may be the result of a lack of information, but it is also the result of different understandings of evidence and how and why we can know that something works. Health professionals, we suggest, traditionally work largely in the positivist tradition, and rely on this type of evidence, namely numbers and what they view as facts. This is, however, changing slowly as the next generation of doctors and health professionals learns about phenomenology or interpretivism at university. As community professionals, we need to be better at promoting the value of *our* kind of evidence and better at making sure we provide the evidence *they* value as well. The following example from a voluntary sector professional working with health colleagues in the public sector illustrates the problem well.

Liz's role was to improve links between health and social care professionals and groups and activities taking place in the community. She became aware that, although these professionals talked very enthusiastically about the benefits of getting involved in community groups, in practice they did not tend to make many referrals to them. Eventually, Liz asked about this lack of referrals in a meeting. In response, some people talked about problems of quality assurance: how do we know the groups are run properly, are there appropriate safeguards in place? Others said they were not sure of the evidence of the benefits of these groups, so were reluctant to refer people to them. Liz asked what kind of evidence they would like to see. Although they agreed that it would be difficult for a community group to demonstrate its impact on health in the same way as a surgical operation or a course of medication, they did not have a clear idea of what an alternative, valid basis for evidence might be. Liz took it on as one of her key roles in this multi-agency group to help them develop a better understanding of evidence that is led by observation.

As well as valuing the understandings of the observer in the generation of knowledge, observation places value on the voices of the observed or participants. In this sense, the knowledge that comes out of observation is co-produced. There is much discussion from those working in and with communities of the importance of the co-production of services. Co-produced services are services that are produced and managed together by traditional service providers (usually the public sector) and communities. Co-production of services can only work, however, if there is an understanding of the co-production of knowledge on which these services are based. We must therefore work with more positivist partners to increase this understanding.

This valuing of different kinds of knowledge has implications for the broader connections between knowledge and power.

We may have all heard the claim that knowledge is power. This claim is a bit of a cliché and like most clichés means less (or at least less clearly) than at first appears to be the case. In fact, different kinds of knowledge have different kinds of power, and there are different definitions and understandings of power. Knowledge, as understood within the positivist tradition, is generally more valued and, therefore, arguably has more power, than the knowledge as understood within the phenomenological or interpretivist tradition. As community workers, we generally work within this latter framework, supporting those who have often been excluded from the production of knowledge to have a voice. Observation is key to this production and therefore a central part of who we are as community workers.

Anecdotes

The phrase 'Well, it's only anecdotal but …' is one that we have probably all heard and many of us have used. Anecdotal evidence is someone's personal story or testimony and is most often contrasted with scientific evidence. It is usually valued as 'only anecdotal' because it may not be justifiable outside of that person's experience. If I said I had met aliens in my back garden, this testimony probably should not be taken that there are aliens in my back garden. It could, however, be taken as evidence that I had experienced (assuming my honesty) a meeting with aliens in my back garden. The positivist would dismiss this testimony as not saying anything meaningful about an objective external reality and they would be right. The phenomenologist or interpretivist, however, is interested in establishing truths about an external world separate from our own experiencing of it and would be interested.

Anecdote is really a subset of observation. It may be something that we observe or something that is reported to us in the course of our practice. It differs from much observation in that it is isolated and not part of an ongoing process. As part of such a process, patterns in observations can be established, providing a robust basis for evidence. The following case study is typical of much anecdotal reporting in which the anecdotal evidence is compelling but not part of a process of research.

Paresh supports a rural development project for workers in southern India, in an area which suffers from steady outward migration. The population has declined by almost 50% in as many years, with those remaining generally living hand to mouth.

Paresh's project aims to bring indigenous knowledge and local organisations together to explore how to make the community and way of life a legitimate option for rural young people who have often felt they had no choice but to leave in search of employment. In the evenings, at the project, workers from the local community received an evening meal and adult learning support in exchange for their contribution to discussions about the community, traditional ways of life and sustainable rural development.

Paresh knew that the project was making a difference, not least because of the high attendance levels and dedicated support from the workers, but also because the local organisations' employers were giving positive feedback about their workers and were beginning to support the project financially. He also heard, from the primary school teachers attached to the project, that the children of those who attended were engaging better since their parents had joined the project.

Anecdotes by definition can not be part of such a pattern of evidence. They do, however, form an important part of the triangulation of evidence and in particular can be a crucial expression of experience that is missed by other kinds of evidence. The importance of this expression was brought home to me on a recent piece of work that my co-author, Ed Garrett, was involved with. I was doing some engagement work on an older people's charter. We were talking about healthcare and support as people move towards the end of their lives, with the unstated assumption that such support was a good thing. An older woman in her mid-eighties then said that she did not necessarily want this kind of continued support. It was not that she was seriously ill, it was just that life felt different to her at this age. Most professionals working with older people are, of course, not in their mid-eighties and will have no direct experience of what this really means. It is important to take seriously this type of expression of personal experience about which none of the professionals sitting around that table could have any direct understanding. It may not have fitted a pattern of evidence, but it was an expression of what life felt like, lived from the inside, and as such is invaluable.

Observation is a way of evidencing impact that is distinctive of (although of course not limited to) those working in and with communities. As practitioners, we must develop the skills to use observation well; essentially, we must have confidence in our own professional judgement. In doing so, we will be addressing some of the linked issues of power, knowledge and voice that at a theoretical level challenge inequality and disadvantage.

Challenge questions

1. How reliable are your observations? How can you manage this?
2. What support do you need to use observation effectively?
3. What assumptions do you use when you reflect on and write up observations?
4. Are you a positivist or a phenomenologist/interpretivist and how does this influence what you think about evidence?

References

Iacono, J., Brown, A. and Holtham, C. (2009) Research methods: a case example of participant observation, *The Electronic Journal of Business Research Methods*, 7(1): 39–46.

Lopez-Dicastillo, O. and Belintxon, M. (2014) The challenges of participant observations of cultural encounters within an ethnograhpic study, *Procedia: Social and Behavioral Sciences*, 132: 522–6.

Shah, A. (2017) Ethnography? Participant observation, a potentially revolutionary praxis, *HAU: Journal of Ethnographic Theory*, 7(1): 45–59.

Taylor-Powell, E. and Steele, S. (1996) *Collecting Evaluation Data: Direct Observation*, Madison, WI: Cooperative Extension Publications, University of Wisconsin.

Wittgenstein, L. (1953) *Philosophical Investigations* (3rd edn, trans. G.E.M Anscombe), Oxford: Blackwell.

Zhao, M. and Ji, Y. (2014) Challenges of introducing participant observation to community health research, *ISRN Nursing*, 2014(802490).

7

Questionnaires

Karen McArdle and Kirsty Forrester

Introduction

This chapter discusses the use of questionnaires as a means of generating evidence of impact. Questionnaires are often used in semi-structured interviews as a schedule of questions and this is discussed further in Chapter 8. Here, we focus on questionnaires completed by the participant or stakeholder. The first thing to mention in thinking about questionnaires is that they rely very much on the willingness of people to give their time, and on literacy issues of comfort with reading and writing. Many a time we have seen people struggling to fill in a questionnaire holding pen or pencil uncomfortably and managing one or two words, if any. As the process is quite distinct, in this chapter we use the term respondents rather than participants, the latter word used elsewhere for learners, clients, patients and other service users.

Robson (2017) makes the following observations on questionnaires:

> Questionnaires are very widely used in small-scale evaluations.... It appears deceptively straightforward to devise the questions. Completion of the questions does not take long and can be incorporated without undue difficulty into a program. Without

forethought, the task of analysis can be routinized and it can generate satisfying quantitative data.

There are some underlying problems, however. Good questionnaires are not easy to devise, as is testified by the prevalence of many awful examples. More fundamentally, the choice of a questionnaire should be governed by the research questions. So, if for example the main purpose of an evaluation is to assess whether the program goals have been achieved, then you only use a questionnaire if it will help to do this. (Robson, 2017, p 104)

This extract describes how the use of questionnaires may appear to be a simple method, but we argue in this chapter that it takes considerable skill to produce a questionnaire that will help you find out what you want to know. Questionnaires are designed mainly – but not exclusively – to supply quantitative information – information in numbers. This chapter does not deal with statistics, as it would require a whole book to do this, but there are many accessible texts suggested for further reading in Box 7.1 at the end of this chapter if you wish to use more than descriptive statistics and basic percentages. Most studies of impact are sufficient with descriptive statistics, but the suggested texts will help if you wish to show causal relationships (cause and effect), and degrees of significance. This is not a chapter on how to do survey research. It is instead a chapter on how to use questionnaires for impact studies. We draw from a range of modern texts in this chapter, but we have chosen to draw in particular from Oppenheim's (1966) *Questionnaire Design and Attitude Measurement*, which we have found to be a very informative, seminal text.

Pros and cons

Thinking about the pros and cons of questionnaires, one advantage is that they are convenient for the designer of small-scale studies, as they involve little work beyond preparing the questions and reading the returned questionnaires. However, they are not a good means of getting rich and in-depth information, as they rely on the respondent supplying such information, which will skew your findings in favour of those who feel comfortable with this means of communication. Questionnaires that rely on selecting emoticons (icons that portray the respondent's moods or facial expressions) to get around literacy issues are, in our opinion, worthless, as they measure very little; we return to this later in this chapter, when we consider the question of exactly what you wish to measure. Questionnaires may seem an exciting, tempting and quick activity for gathering information, but they are frequently misleading and have faults that make them invalid and deceptive. This may sound negative, but this is because questionnaires are often very badly designed and used for the wrong reasons. By the end of this chapter, we hope to have given you the confidence to design questionnaires correctly and effectively.

Questionnaires are particularly good if the study is a large-scale study of impact, as they are a good means of getting information from a large population. They are somewhat limited in the quality of information they can secure, but they can be triangulated with other methods, such as focus groups or interviews, and provide a picture across a wide spectrum. If you present a one-off training programme to a dozen people, you are unlikely to find a follow-up questionnaire useful, as it will tell you very little. You would be better off asking people about the programme directly or leaving the room and asking them to discuss it and nominate a spokesperson to give you feedback. If, however, you are interested in an employability programme involving 150 people, for example, a questionnaire will be a very useful means of finding out about it. The following case study provides an example of positive use of a questionnaire.

A questionnaire was used by a community group for a project in a neighbourhood of Aberdeen. The group sought two things. First of all, it wanted to assess learning needs for a community centre, and second, it wanted to assess whether the current provision of the centre was having a positive impact on the community. There were approximately 300 households in the community, and the group decided to deliver a questionnaire to each household. A nearby university provided a grant to conduct the study and a university staff member designed the questionnaire in consultation with the community group. A questionnaire was selected as the most appropriate means of gathering information because the community wanted to cover the whole area and include all residents in the data. This was balanced against the difficulty that some of the population does not have English as their first language or may have literacy difficulties. To address this issue, community centre volunteers provided language assistance to help respondents complete the questionnaire. The amount of data generated was extensive and was managed using SPSS (Statistical Package for the Social Sciences) software. The questionnaire used open questions to find out why people were not inclined to use the centre and found, among other things, that it had a reputation of being only for mothers and toddlers. Those who did use the centre knew a member of the community committee and were therefore familiar with the range of activities offered. This provided a starting point for the community committee to consider its plans for the next three years.

Another positive point about questionnaires is that they enable you to quantify information. This is important because numbers are valued highly in fields such as politics or the media. Moreover, being able to state that 80% of people benefit from a service may be useful, but also raises questions about the other 20%. Questionnaires are often used to assess need – door knocking to see if there is a need for a particular resource. We then, however, encounter the problem that people may think about attending a service or event, but when their favourite programme is on the television or dinner needs making, good intentions fly out of the window. We return later to the subject of the credibility of answers to questionnaires.

In the Aberdeen case study mentioned earlier, the questionnaire found that community spirit was very high in a relatively disadvantaged area, with more than 80% of residents indicating that they liked to live there and many of them ascribing this to 'neighbourliness', friendship and integration of different cultures. This information was used in successful applications for further funding for community activities from the local council.

When to use a questionnaire

You may find a questionnaire a useful means of gathering information in the following circumstances:

- when you have a large population to consult, or people who are at a distance from you (you cannot access them easily);
- when you have fairly straightforward questions to ask;
- when the people you wish to consult are most likely literate;
- when you are dealing with numerical data.

Questionnaire design

Questionnaire design is a complex process and needs careful thought. If you intend to use a questionnaire for a survey, you should first pilot it with a group of people. However good you are at writing, you cannot predict what people will understand, so you need to test the questionnaire with around three to five people. We shall come back to this later.

Questionnaires are designed to measure variables. A variable is an idea that can be measured. So, if you are interested in men and women, the variable is sex. If you are interested in how old they are, the variable is age. If you are interested their opinion of hospital care, the variable is attitude to hospital care. You must think very carefully in measurement terms about each variable you intend to measure; again, we shall return to this later.

Questionnaires have a logical sequence. Like a story, they should have a beginning, middle and end. The first thing to include in your questionnaire is an introduction to what it is about. You will probably include a covering letter or some other kind of explanation when you distribute the questionnaire, but it is good to have a welcoming sentence at the beginning of the questionnaire itself. Whether you include the demographic questions (about sex, age, residential location, ethnicity and so on) at the beginning or end is a contested decision. Some people believe you should start with easy demographic questions to get the respondent started. Others think a more interesting question is helpful at the start and prefer to leave the demographic questions to the end when the respondent may be more tired. The most important thing is to sequence questions logically and naturally. If you are looking for in-depth answers, build up to them. Think about how the respondent's mind will be working in the questionnaire. Are you asking them to dodge all over the place with answers, or is there a logical sequence for their thoughts?

It is important, at the end of the questionnaire, to thank the respondent for their answers and for taking the time to complete the questionnaire. You should also include details of how and where to return the completed questionnaire. In laying out your questionnaire, you will naturally have left room for the coding process that will take place during data analysis. Data analysis is discussed later in this chapter. You should not, of course, ask respondents for their name and address, however much you may want to. Given that questionnaires are about impact, responses must be anonymous to guarantee unbiased answers. It is important not to try to fool people by numbering the questionnaires so that you can track them – this is bad practice.

You should also be careful in your design not to overload the respondent. Twenty questions, for example, would constitute a long questionnaire. We usually aim for no more than six open questions, with the remainder being closed questions. It is important for our discussion that you know the difference between open and closed questions. For an open question, a respondent can give any answer she or he chooses, and for a closed question, the answers are limited, as the following examples show:

- Closed question: Are you a resident of Nashville?
  - Yes
  - No

- * Prefer not to say
- Closed question: Do you like:
  - * horse riding?
  - * cycling?
  - * reading?
- Open question: Where do you live?
- Open question: What is your favourite hobby?

Most questionnaires consist of both kinds of questions. As you can see from the examples, closed questions can be attitudinal as well as factual. It is important to be very careful in selecting the responses we offer. If we ask the question, 'Some people in the community have too much power. Who are they?', some people might think in term of political parties, others in terms of criminals, and others in terms of professional groups such as doctors and lawyers, for example. So, in this case it would probably be better to use an open question. Closed questions, however, are quicker and easier to answer and they do not require high literacy (Oppenheim, 1966). The disadvantage of closed questions is the loss of spontaneity and expressiveness on the part of the respondent. The respondent is 'forced' to choose between given alternatives and think of alternatives they may not otherwise have considered.

The most important feature of questionnaire design is knowing what you want to find out. You should carefully consider what ending you would put at the end of the sentence beginning: 'What I really want to know is …'. This will lead you to your variables, which are crucial for both question design and analysis of data. So if your completed sentence is 'I really want to know about attitude to the nursing staff in the community in relation to wound dressing', one of your variables is likely to be sex of nursing staff; another is wound dressing; and a third is attitude to wound-dressing procedure. You will probably have many other variables, but this gives you a start.

Overall, questionnaire design is aimed at precision, exactness and efficiency. It is not a quick and easy method of finding out about impact. It requires, care, attention and exactitude, as well as patience and a deliberate attitude, but when you get it right it can be very pleasing.

Attitudes

Examining attitudes means exploring thoughts and feelings. Given that we are looking for evidence of impact, we are likely to want to explore attitudes rather than just facts. Attitudes are also beliefs that may attract strong feelings and a likelihood of behaving in particular ways. They are, of course, conceptual and not factual, however real they may feel to the individual answering the questions.

In questionnaires, the approach to attitudes may be rather primitive (Oppenheim, 1966). Attitudes tend to be perceived as straight lines from positive, through neutral, to negative feelings about the object in question, and we place a person's attitude on a linear continuum so it can be measured in a numerical way. This does not do attitudes justice. As Oppenheim (1966) suggests, attitudes may be shaped more like concentric circles or three-dimensional cloud formations.

The degree of differentiation at one end of an attitude continuum may be different from that at the other end. Taking peace as an example, it is easy to think about war, courage and bravery but more difficult to think about another end to the continuum without reference to negatives such as the absence of fighting or lack of need for courage. Similarly, intervals at one end of a continuum may be smaller or more numerous than at the other end.

Attitudes are complex and interrelated as well as not being linear, so prejudice against one group of people is likely to be associated with prejudice against other groups, for example. We cannot isolate attitudes to any great extent, and nor do attitudes necessarily constitute a balanced view after careful consideration. Some attitudes are intensely felt and deeply entrenched in our belief system, whereas others are just preferences and may not endure. It is almost impossible to discover these nuances from a questionnaire.

It is therefore important to think very carefully about exactly what we wish to measure. We must analyse complexities and interrelationships so we can be sure we are measuring what we think we are measuring. Piloting the questionnaire is crucial to make sure you have got it right, as is maintaining a relationship with your respondents. You should always explain how they were chosen for the survey, stress confidentiality and never ask questions that make them feel they are wrong in their opinion.

Question design

> Some people still design questions as if the process of interviewing or of filling out a questionnaire were rather like unloading a ship, with every item of cargo labeled [sic] and with a specific destination, picked out of the hold and set down according to a pattern. In reality, questioning people is more like trying to catch a particularly elusive fish, by hopefully casting different kinds of bait at different depths, without knowing what goes on beneath the surface! (Oppenheim, 1966, p 49)

The function of a question is to elicit a particular communication. We hope that our respondents have attitudes on the subject of our inquiry, and we want to evoke these attitudes with a minimum of distortion. We must therefore design our questions very carefully. People's attitudes may be clear and well organised, or diffuse and vague. They may be deep or superficial, latent or very strongly held (Oppenheim, 1966). Our opinion of a service provided may be quite straightforward or entangled with complex emotions. What is uppermost in the respondent's mind may not amount to a fair representation of their collected thoughts on the subject, so some process of awareness inevitably takes place – self-analysis, feedback, conceptualisation of ideas and generalisation on specific points. These processes may be affected by a number of things – such as wishful thinking that the ideas will come right, a desire to please the community worker, a desire to 'look good', or merely puzzlement. Respondents may also have memory problems, so questions must be designed well to minimise these factors.

Having already considered questionnaire design, we should have a plan of the sequence of minor and major variables. It is then a question of considering each variable in turn and deciding how thoroughly we want to investigate it. We shall begin with thinking about factual questions, so called because they do not deal with the complexities of knowledge, motives and attitudes. It is important use language carefully in all questions, but it is easy to forget this in the case of factual questions.

Language in questions

Another requirement in framing questions is to be mindful of different interpretations of the same ideas. In the UK, for example, people have different understandings of the words 'dinner' and 'tea', depending on which part of the country they come from. Similarly, in studies of housing, people typically report fewer bedrooms than they actually have for the reason that they do not consider a study or sewing room or playroom to be a bedroom. Again, the word 'family' means different things depending on one's frame of reference. It could mean the nuclear family or wider extended family, for example, and the term may not apply at all in the context of children in care.

You should ensure that your respondents understand the language of the questions by avoiding jargon or concepts with multiple interpretations. It is no good asking individuals if they feel empowered when this is a complex idea that will have different meanings for different people, if indeed they understand it at all. Similarly, you need to be very thoughtful in designing questions for children and young people, who may use different terms from adults. Be aware, however, that the colloquial language of young people, while very up-to-date, may not be used by all young people, and that young people are not a homogenous group, as the following example shows:

> Donald consulted young people in a youth club to help design a questionnaire for other young people. He wanted the young people to have control of the process and he asked them to design the questions, so that the language and ideas would be accessible to young people. The young people devised closed questions about the desirability of a skate park and places to 'just hang out'. A supervisor was rightly

concerned that the only respondents would be those who were interested in such activities and that the consultation would not appeal to young people who liked art, crafts, music or reading, for example.

We must also be wary of assuming that people have the information we choose to ask them for. If a question involves remembering something, we are assuming that the respondent will recall the information accurately. We all process memories, which become stories that may be considered truthful to the teller but may not represent cold, hard facts.

Leading and loaded questions

Leading questions are questions that are not neutral. 'Most people believe in equal opportunities in employment today; do you?' is an obviously leading question, but they can be more subtle, such as 'Are you against giving power to children in schools?'. A loaded question is one that is emotionally coloured and suggests automatic approval or disapproval. Examples include motherhood, of which most people approve, or poverty, of which most people disapprove. You can overcome this by avoiding such words and by paraphrasing instead. Sometimes we lead people by failing to create the opportunity for giving certain answers. For example, the question 'Would you prefer to be counselled by a man?' does not allow the option of saying 'I don't mind whether it is a man or woman'.

Prestige bias is common in some kinds of survey and should be avoided. Many factual questions are loaded with prestige leading to bias. For example, Oppenheim (1966) reports that people claim they brush their teeth more often than is likely, and we would add that in surveys many people routinely underestimate how much they drink or smoke. There is no simple answer to this; just be aware of it. Similarly, if you phrase a question with the words 'Doctors say …', people are more likely to agree with the question because of the social standing and presumed knowledge of doctors. This would be the same for questions that begin 'Research has shown …'. This can be avoided quite easily by not using this type of phraseology.

Checklists, rating scales and other structures for responses

Closed questions allow the individual to respond without writing too much, but in many cases the answers provide very limited insight.

> Often such techniques look impressive and 'scientific' in a questionnaire but we must maintain a critical attitude and ask ourselves what this set of questions is trying to achieve, and how the results will be used.
> (Oppenheim, 1966, p 82)

This quotation warns against the 'scientific' look of a questionnaire, which can be quite misleading. Checklists ask respondents to rate attributes along the lines of 'very important', 'important', 'not important' and 'don't know', for example. It is not always clear what one can do with this kind of information. What does it actually mean?

The following checklist asks what you consider to be desirable qualities in a partner by rating the qualities as 'very important' through to 'not important':

- financially solvent
- attractive
- kind
- generous
- interested in children
- good at keeping the house clean
- good sense of humour

In questions like this, it is important to be clear whether you want to know about the respondent and their preferences in a partner, or whether you want to know about the qualities and how often they are preferred. This kind of question is better for the latter than the former, as it is framed simply and people are very complex.

Ratings give a numerical value to some kind of judgement. The idea is that respondents allocate so many marks out of, say,

10 or 100, or increasingly, in computerised questionnaires, to use a sliding scale to move a marker to a preferred position. This is fraught with danger, as people are often asked to rate things such as a service without due regard to change in perception over time or experiences on different occasions. There is also an inherent assumption that we can judge complex services using a number, and that the numbers given mean the same level of regard to different individuals. The following example shows the potential flaws of using such ratings.

> Donald used a sliding scale on a social media site in his young people's consultation to find out how often people used the youth club but the question asked was quite complex, and it was unclear whether the slider referred to attendance in weeks, months or years, so the results were flawed. Some people slid the marker to 10 and others chose 1, but it was impossible to judge frequency. The people who chose 10 might just have meant that they used the youth club a lot.

Another consideration is the 'halo effect', whereby respondents rate things according to their overall feeling of like or dislike for them, rather than looking at each individual item in a rating scale. One way of avoiding this is to put the rating questions on different pages of the questionnaire and keep them to a minimum. Moreover, there is a limit to the number of ratings, rankings or checklists you can include in questionnaire without respondents getting bored, so it is important to avoid filling more than a page with such items, if, indeed, they are all presented together. Rankings sometimes tells us more about respondents and their overall feelings for a topic than about the ranking of individual items, even though the latter is the intention of the exercise.

An inventory is a list of things that respondents are asked to mark in a particular way, such as activities that interested them, for example. Grids or matrices are a form of inventory that require respondents to check across two dimensions.

In the example in Table 7.1, respondents (elderly people) are asked to indicate whether they have experienced an ailment against who they consulted about it.

Table 7.1: Example matrix inventory

	Family	Nurse	Pharmacist	Doctor	Hospital accident and emergency department
Cold					
Blocked ears					
Bed sore					
Chest pain					
Memory problems					
Flu					
Holiday vaccinations					

Finally, Likert scales are probably the most relevant and frequently used type of closed question, and comprise a series of statements ranging from 'strongly agree', through intermediate stages such as 'agree', 'don't know' and 'disagree', to 'strongly disagree'. You will almost certainly be familiar with these. The cautions we have proposed before apply equally to these questions. What exactly does 'agree' mean? How much is 'strongly'? Such scales can be used to get a general sense of agreement about a statement over large populations, but tell us very little in a small population.

The statements used in Likert scales should be carefully constructed; you should avoid using leading statements or statements that are all positive or all negative. Sentence completion is also a form of attitude study that is commonly used in questionnaires and you should take particular care to avoid leading questions and those that make assumptions. The following example shows the pitfalls of sentence completion.

As part of his youth consultation, Donald asked young people to complete the sentence: 'What I would like the community centre to do is ...'. He made two assumptions in his question design. The first was that the respondent would indeed want the centre to do something. The second implicit assumption was that respondents would attend the activity they suggested.

Coding of data

In designing your questionnaire, you will have left a margin at the right-hand side of the page for your codes for the answers given. Once you receive the completed questionnaires, you will prepare a code book, assigning a number to each of the answers in the closed questions. For the open questions, you will review a sample and ascribe codes to the commonly mentioned answers for the purposes of numerical analysis. You may also make a note of any interesting answers to use as illustrative quotations. You will then code each questionnaire for data entry on a computer or for simple, manual calculation. You will need to add to your codes for open questions if answers arise that you have not predicted. Coding allows entry to simple statistical packages; alternatively, you can analyse by hand. You should read each questionnaire in full to get a picture of the person responding, as well as analysing the answers across the questionnaire by question number. You will have common numbers across questions for blank and 'don't know' answers, or for those you are unable to decipher.

Once this is done, you can make simple descriptive accounts of your findings or enter the data into a computerised statistical package. The advantage of using a statistical package is that it can manage large volumes of data and generate statistical analyses with charts and graphs. Up to around 80 questionnaires with ten to 15 questions are just about manageable by hand if you want simple, descriptive statistics such as percentages, mode, mean and median, but it is worth using a computer if you have large amounts of data, even though data entry can be time-consuming and very boring, and requires total accuracy.

Interpretation of data is very important in using questionnaires, so that you can ascribe meaning to the numbers presented. Simple statistics of correlation can be calculated by hand. Numbers are rather bland and need explanation. Be very cautious about how you use statistics beyond simple counts, and of ascribing cause and effect without an understanding of statistical processes. That being said, it is possible to produce an attractive report with graphs and simple statistics derived from questionnaires.

There are many accessible texts on statistics if you wish explore the topic further. Box 7.1 mentions three that we have found particularly useful.

Box 7.1 Further reading on statistics

Cramer, D. and Howitt, D. (2004) *The Sage Dictionary of Statistics*, London: Sage.

Rowntree, D. (2000) *Statistics Without Tears: An Introduction for Non-Mathematicians*, London: Penguin.

Schacht, S. (2018) *Social and Behavioral Statistics: A User-Friendly Approach*, New York, NY: Routledge.

Challenge questions

1. Why would you wish to use a questionnaire?
2. Is a questionnaire the best form of data gathering for your study of impact?
3. With whom do you intend to pilot your questionnaire?
4. What other forms of impact data do you intend to gather for triangulation?
5. Are numbers the best way of describing the impact of what you do?

References

Oppenheim, A.N. (1966) *Questionnaire Design and Attitude Measurement*, London: Heinemann.

Robson, C. (2017) *Small-Scale Evaluation: Principles and Practice* (2nd edn), London: Sage.

8

Interviews and focus groups

Karen McArdle, Kirsty Forrester and Ed Garrett

Introduction

This chapter combines discussion of interviews and focus groups because they are both face-to-face means of gathering evidence of effectiveness. They are perhaps the most exciting means of gathering evidence, as the evidence comes directly from participants, who often have the most telling methods of letting us know exactly what they think about what we do.

We begin by thinking about metaphors that go with generating evidence by asking questions. Such metaphors include 'extracting information', 'digging for ideas' or 'mining for data' and are very one-sided, in that they refer to the person gathering data rather than the person who is providing it. They also assume there is a 'truth' residing in the interviewee that can be foraged out. We contend that any conversation or interview is a social dialogue in which meaning is constructed between people; it is never one-sided. People are social beings and always construct meaning together; this we suggest, demands metaphors of 'building', 'developing ideas' and 'working together'. We propose that information generated in interviews is not a found 'true' answer to a question, but rather a co-construction of reality between two people. This means that awareness of both self and reflexivity on the part of the interviewer are crucial. For example, individuals interviewed about attitudes to pre-marital sex may give different answers or different slants to their opinion depending on the age of the interviewer. We return to reflexivity and self-awareness later in this chapter and we refer you to Chapter 15 on self-evaluation.

Engaging with people for interviews is very important if you wish to get more than just phatic or polite answers to questions. The interviewee in an interview situation is often expected to give all the words. We suggest that this is a gift of ideas from the interviewee and that it demands reciprocity. Engaging with the interviewee, and giving a bit of yourself, is a very effective means of doing this, and is a natural part of any conversation. It also equalises the implicit power dynamic of interviewer and interviewee. It can be done quite simply, by 'giving' an account of your journey to the interview, for example. Was the traffic heavy? Was it raining? Did you forget your umbrella? This is a simple way of giving of your own experience, which is something you are going to ask the interviewee to do.

We are not suggesting that you become the friend of the interviewee. You must have boundaries around what you share to avoid influencing the interviewee's responses. You are not, however, going to derive the desired information if you act like a research automaton. You will probably get superficial clipped responses if you act as the objective external researcher. Finding a balance is important, as the sympathetic and empathetic explorer who is interested in the ideas of others in general and the interviewee in particular. You will be approaching the interview with your own assumptions about what is right and wrong, and the lens through which you view the world must be finely honed so that you see things in a relatively neutral light and accept all answers as a 'truth' and as worthwhile. This is achieved through reflexivity.

> Neil was doing a study of what made people volunteer for the elderly people's charity with which he worked. He asked ten people what their motivation was for participating in the work of the charity. One of the interviewees said he wanted more business contacts and to network to further his business interests as a financial adviser. Neil told a colleague this and said that the interview had been

irritating. The colleague suggested that Neil consider why he thought this person irritating; was he making assumptions about the person based on his own idea about what was right? The colleague suggested that Neil had been biased against the interviewee because of his own views about what should motivate people. Neil went back to the recorded interview with a more open mind and found that the interviewee had other motivations that Neil had missed because he had been irritated by the business motivation. Neil needed to be reflexive and analyse the lens he was using to interpret what he found out. The lens through which Neil saw the world had been affected by Neil's worldview.

Planning interviews

Interviews are used because they generally, if conducted properly, provide rich data and manage the complexity of the ideas sought. They give a first-hand account of experience and are usually interesting and relatively easy to conduct. They do not require a large sample because validity is dependent on the depth not breadth of information. They do, however, have disadvantages in that they may be considered to be biased if they are conducted by a professional who is well known to the interviewee. This can be overcome by using an external interviewer or by being rigorous about the questions asked and prompting and probing for genuine opinions. We return to this later in the chapter.

When planning an interview, you should first decide how many people to interview. If you have a project with eight people in it, you will probably interview all of them. With a project with 50 people, you may interview just ten of them, but you will have to be clear about the criteria you use to select them. It may be important to have different sexes represented. You may choose some older and some younger participants. You may choose those who have been at the project a long time. Whatever you do, you should be explicit about how you choose your participants. Sometimes, it is quite clear that you need to be purposive and choose people who are well able to offer an

The Impact of Community Work

opinion. For a project on young people with autism, mentioned in Chapter 4, author Karen McArdle chose to interview those with more developed speech. To ensure that the study was not biased, she also observed those without speech during the project activities to get an impression of their experience.

There are decisions to be made about where to conduct interviews. It is usual and courteous to accommodate the interviewee rather than expecting them to come to you. The location should be quiet and private. Privacy is important, as standard ethical practice demands that you guarantee confidentiality. The timing of the interview needs careful consideration. Will it be before, in the middle of, or after an intervention? You will get different answers depending on whether you interview on a Monday morning or a Friday evening.

Exactly what you are going to ask depends on the type of interview you intend to conduct – structured, semi-structured or unstructured. A structured interview make uses of questionnaires (see Chapter 7). This involves you reading out the questions, and the potential answers in the case of closed questions, and writing down exactly what is said. This allows you to gain numerical answers, as all interviewees experience the questionnaire read out in the same way. Semi-structured interviews enable prompting – suggesting a choice of answers from a pre-determined list – and probing, or asking for more information: 'Can you tell me more about that?', 'Can you give me an example of that?'. Semi-structured interviews also follow a pre-designed format and are intended to be the same for everyone. Unstructured interviews are designed to follow a more natural conversational format. You will have prepared a schedule containing questions, but you may wish to diverge from the order of questions to allow the conversation to flow more naturally. We discussed questionnaire design in Chapter 7 and the same principles apply to interview schedules, apart from the schedule for an unstructured interview, which will contain the topics you wish to cover and suggested questions you might ask to keep the conversation flowing. The following is an example of a schedule for an unstructured interview about the quality of a leadership training programme:

1. Introductions and ethical statement of confidentiality.
2. Motivation for training programme:
   • What made you decide to attend the programme?
3. Experience of the programme:
   • What did you like most about the programme?
   • What did you like least about the programme?
4. Learning:
   • What did you learn in the course of the programme?
   • How did the programme affect your practice?
5. Take-away learning:
   • Did the programme have relevance to your practice?
   • Will the programme affect how you work in future?
6. Feelings:
   • How did you feel in the course of the training?
   • How do you feel now about the training?
7. Conclusions:
   • Would you recommend this course to other people?
   • Close and thanks.

Conducting interviews

Most interviewees are used to being interviewed. They will expect you to ask them a series of questions, and are likely to give relatively short answers without much thought. If you wish for more than this from your interview, you should engage well with your participant and ensure that the interview becomes more like a conversation. This means behaving in a way that is accepting and acknowledges all answers to your questions. Your body language should be affirming whether or not you agree with what is being said. This means nodding and making eye contact and agreeing sounds – just saying 'yes' is sufficient. If you disagree with something, you do not have to lie – nodding and affirming the right to have an opinion is sufficient. There are many ways in which you can affirm what people say and it is difficult in text to represent these, but concentrating on being accepting and affirming is appropriate unless you are distressed by the interviewee crossing certain boundaries. For example, racism should not be tolerated in most circumstances, and it is acceptable to disagree with racist comments in a polite and effective manner. If abuse or exploitation is revealed or you feel that your interviewee is at risk of harm, it is your duty by law in many countries to report this to the relevant authorities.

Interviews vary in length. An in-depth interview potentially lasts for an hour or more, but an interview about the effectiveness of a programme should not last for more than 20 minutes to half an hour.

Self-awareness and reflexivity

We mentioned earlier in this chapter that the lens through which, you, as the interviewer, view the world should be clear to you, as it will affect how you analyse and interpret what you hear. As practitioners, whenever we plan to conduct interviews, it is always good practice to ensure that we are asked the questions ourselves. It is a simple matter to ask someone to run through the interview schedule with you as the interviewee. This enables you to discover your own assumptions about what is 'right' and you will see the lens through which you will be viewing your interviewees. This can be very illuminating exercise and it is interesting to see how your opinion of an intervention differs from that of your participants, assuming you are doing your own interviewing for a project.

External interviewers

An external interviewer is arguably more objective and may discover things that the interviewee is afraid or embarrassed to tell you. You should balance this against the advantage you have over an external interviewer in being able to get beyond the 'polite' stage, as you will already have engaged with the participants. It has often been suggested that participants may seek to please an interviewer who has been a friend in the programme, and that this is potentially problematic. Even if this is the case, a pre-existing relationship challenges the interviewer to genuinely probe and explore the true picture of people's experience through balanced questions that look for both good and bad experiences. It is of paramount importance, therefore, that the interviewer be aware of and consider power dynamics carefully when planning and carrying out interviews. The following case study provides an example of seeking the right balance between using an external interviewer or someone already involved in the project to conduct interviews:

> Brian works in public health and wants more detail on the impact of a lunch club for older people funded by the public health provider. He decides to use interviews as the main way to provide evidence of this impact, but not to do the interviews himself, as he does not know the lunch club members at all and he is aware of the position of power he holds as a health professional. He thinks a better relationship of trust will give more interesting and honest results. He initially thinks of asking the lunch club volunteers to do the interviews but wonders whether the club members would be entirely open with the volunteers, especially about aspects of the club they might not like. He decides instead to approach members of a local older people's forum to do the interviews. They know the members but are not actually involved in the club. The older people's forum members interview the lunch club members at the end of a lunch club session while they are having coffee. This relaxed, informal atmosphere means the members really open up about what the lunch club means to them.

Balanced questions

In Chapter 7, we discussed the pitfalls of using leading questions. It is perfectly possible to conduct an interview in which the only possible answers are positive ones. The questions need to be balanced and actively seek negative experiences or feelings as well as positive ones, so be sure to ask about things people did not enjoy or that provoked negative emotions.

Is it important to be clear about what you want to know. This relies on the theory behind what you do as a practitioner. For example, our theory of learning concerns the transformation of the individual from one state of knowledge, skills and experience to another. So, in interviews we seek evidence of such transformation, but do not use this language; instead, we talk about learning. If you work in the health domain and seek change in the experience of health and wellbeing, or change in health-linked behaviour, for example, your questions should reflect this.

It is important to be clear about exactly what you want to find out. We have seen many interview schedules for learning programmes that ask about the quality of the lunch or the room in which the learning took place. We consider such questions to be a waste of useful time unless the answers are a priority for the consideration of impact. Yes, the room and lunch may affect learning, but let the participant tell you this unprompted if this is the case. In any event, we suggest that such details are relatively low on the list of priorities for impact and can be judged by a group facilitator, rather than the interviewer using precious interview time for practicalities that will emerge unprompted if they are important enough.

Focus groups

> Being in groups is a common experience. We find ourselves invited, herded or seduced into groups for planning, decision making, advising, brainstorming, learning, sharing or self-help. Groups can be fun and fruitful but they can also be agonizing experiences that are unnecessary, unproductive and time consuming. (Krueger and Casey, 2009, p 1)

Krueger and Casey go on to suggest that the two reasons group experiences turn into wasted time are that the group leader is 'fuzzy' about the purpose; and loses control of the group. Focus groups rely heavily on group process skills and on clarity of purpose. Focus groups are intended to gather opinions. They are used to get people to talk to each other. Participants are selected because they have certain things in common, such as having had the same experience or service. The facilitator of the group creates a 'permissive' environment (Kruger and Casey,

2009) to share perceptions and points of view. Participants should not be asked to vote or reach consensus, as the purpose of the group is not to reach decisions but to find out. Focus groups are a useful means of needs assessment. Needs are often complex and multifaceted and focus groups can help disentangle these needs. Focus groups allow people to reflect on the opinions of others.

Focus groups work well because participants are often more willing to express themselves when others do the same. They are also a more practical method of getting the views of a large number of people than one-to-one interviews. Focus groups work well when people feel comfortable and respected. They can be a safe environment for expression of negative views as well as positive views, as people feel more comfortable sharing views that are supported by others.

One of the downsides of focus groups is that some participants may seek to portray themselves in a particular way, such as being an intellectual or a 'mover and shaker'. Competition can emerge to be the cleverest or most active member of a community group. This demands careful management by the facilitator.

Focus groups characteristically comprise around 6 to 12 people, but with skill, when needs must, they can be run with 20 or three participants. We suggest planning for around 10 people. Participants do not necessarily know each other when they meet as they may have been on different programmes, so it is important to tell them what they have in common and, in particular, why they have been selected. In our work on learning as transformation, a focus group will typically last about an hour and a half, but an hour is fine. It is also useful in organisational terms to 'piggyback' on another meeting. If participants are meeting for another purpose, simply ask them to stay for an extra hour to help you with your focus group. Similarly, if you are not sure who to include, use a 'snowballing' technique and ask an individual to bring a friend in the same circumstances.

Clarity of purpose

We have already discussed clarity of purpose for interviews, and the same applies to focus groups. You should decide, first of all, exactly what you want to find out and then make a judgement about whether a focus group is the best method for doing this. Krueger and Casey (2009) suggest using focus groups in the following circumstances, among others:

- when looking for a range of views;
- when seeking differences between groups or categories of people;
- when seeking ideas that are greater than the sum of their parts, where there is synergy;
- where there is value in collecting the comments or language of a population.

It is also important to know when not to use a focus group, for example if the experience and information you wish to collect is sensitive or if the atmosphere in a group is emotionally charged.

Focus group questions

It is crucial to develop good questions. These should be clearly understood and the participants should know the answers. Selecting the right language to use is therefore important; you should avoid jargon and be cognisant of the type of language participants will use themselves. In our practice, we usually make a point of beginning with a simple question to which everyone will know the answer, so that participants become confident and used to speaking in a group. So, for example, we might ask which community people live in or how long they have been involved in the project or organisation in question, and ensure that everyone gives an answer.

Just as with questionnaires and interviews, it is vital to seek a process that is logical and puts difficult issues towards the end when people will have warmed up a bit. Questions should follow a train of thought, so it is important to consider transitions from one line of questioning to another, as well as closing questions that encourage participants to summarise the most important points raised. The interview schedule should look exactly like the one used for an unstructured interview.

The focus group process

We assume that, as practitioners who work or volunteer in the community, you already have group work skills and are well able to facilitate groups. This book is not the place to rehearse these ideas, but it is important here to outline the difference between a focus group and a therapeutic or learning group. The primary purpose of a focus group is to elicit ideas and information; it does not concern the wellbeing of the participants as such, although you should bear this in mind as part of your process. You should be looking for quantity and depth of ideas in a focus group. When conflict of opinion arises, you should listen to the nature of the disagreement rather than try to resolve it or seek consensus. Clearly, it would be preferable if conflict did not arise, but it is not your role to seek to manage this, as you may be suppressing important ideas. You do, however, have a responsibility for the wellbeing of the participants, and this must be balanced against difference of opinion.

Similarly, it is helpful if everyone gives an opinion and it is important that one person does not dominate the whole procedure, but it is not the role of the facilitator to try to alter behaviour in groups. The dominating individual can easily be moderated politely, using words such as, 'Thank you for your input; let's see what others think'. Similarly, it is not your role to ensure that everyone participates equally, although it is important that everyone is invited to contribute. You might say to a quiet person, "Do you have anything to say about this topic, Marie?". The following case study is an example of managing focus groups so that all participants have sufficient opportunity to contribute.

A team of urban planners had received funding to explore what was important to local people when designing urban spaces. They employed a community engagement officer, Piotr, to carry out focus groups. Piotr decided to engage with existing community groups, setting up focus groups with those who were actively involved in community life. The challenge he had was engaging those who did not volunteer or get involved in youth and community groups. As much of the local population was engaged in manufacturing, he managed to set up focus groups at two of the largest local employers. He also visited a local boxing gym and pool hall to try to get voices that were not usually heard. As an outsider, Piotr knew that within all of his focus groups there could be power dynamics of which he would be unaware, so he knew that he would have to rely on his experience and gut feelings when managing the groups.

He sent transcriptions of all the focus group discussions to the participants to give them the opportunity to withdraw or amend their comments. This provided an opportunity for quieter members of the focus groups to express other opinions or confirm those that had been expressed by others.

It is important to record focus groups, as it is difficult to run a group and take notes at the same time. It is good practice to ask permission to use a digital recorder at the beginning, but be prepared, if someone objects, to invite a colleague or friend to take notes. One point here is crucial and this is the ethics of running a focus group. With interviews, you should always guarantee confidentiality and confirm the interviewee's willingness to participate. During the interview, you may well renegotiate the agreement by asking the interviewee if they are happy to continue. In a focus group, you should also ask for informed consent to participate, but confidentiality is much more complex in such settings. All of the group will hear the opinions given, and you cannot guarantee that participants will keep them confidential. Accordingly, it is good practice to negotiate 'keeping opinions in this room', in order to encourage some openness. You should, of course, promise confidentiality in the way you present the opinions of the participants by not using names or identifying features in any subsequent comment or narrative unless agreed with the individual concerned.

Analysis and interpretation of focus groups and interviews

It is crucial to be systematic in your analysis and interpretation of focus groups and interviews. It is not sufficient to consider what you *think* you heard. You should be open to alternatives from what you expect or expected to hear. Two clear processes are helpful in analysing and interpreting data. The first is to check back with participants what you think you heard and the sense you have subsequently made of it. You can do this by sending a copy of what you have written about to all interviewees *before* publishing it to ensure that they agree with your interpretation of their meaning. The second process is to get someone else to look at the transcript of the interview or focus group discussion to find out how they would analyse and interpret it. This is a very helpful way of checking taken-for-granted assumptions. If you had a colleague or friend helping with the focus group, they may be well placed to provide a different interpretation, although it is often preferable that they know nothing about your work in order to avoid 'group-speak' interpretations.

Transcription plays a crucial role in the analysis and interpretation of ideas from participants. This involves listening to your digital recording and writing down every word that has been uttered. There are complex systems for showing pauses and hesitation, but it is sufficient to indicate such breaks in speech by using brackets, as in (pauses) or (laughs). It is best to do this yourself, as you will find yourself interpreting the data as you write, and it is a good way of familiarising yourself with the interviews. It can be time-consuming, but will be well worth the effort. Focus group discussions are notoriously difficult to transcribe, so doing it yourself is the best method, as, having been the facilitator, you will remember what was said in outline. While you are transcribing, be sure to include notes of ideas in your reflective diary, so you do not lose them. If you lack the time to do the transcription, it is vital for your analysis to listen to the recording repeatedly and make detailed notes.

Analysis and interpretation take place at the same time but are also separate procedures. Analysis in this context involves answering some basic questions, as follows:

- What has been confirmed?
- What has been challenged?
  - What is new?
  - What is different from previous thinking?
  - What themes are emerging?
  - What differences of opinion are emerging?
  - What are the similarities between people?
  - What is the nature of any differences?

Some people find diagrams and mind maps to be helpful in showing linkages between ideas and themes to capture complexity. Interpretation is about meanings and you will discover these as you analyse the data. You may also find metaphor helpful in analysing data, as in the example of a colleague who interpreted an interviewee who was finding it hard to reflect on her difficult childhood as shining a lamp from behind frosted glass.

Analysis of both interviews and focus groups always has two facets: what was said, and how it was said. In an interview transcript, you will look at the answers to such questions as outlined in the previous paragraph; at the way in which the answers were expressed, in what order and with what strength; and at what was not said. In focus groups, people agree and disagree; they influence each other; and they moderate and strengthen views based on what other people say. The discussion evolves and is a journey with stops, starts and deviations. You should consider each person's experience of the group process.

Computerised data analysis packages are useful, particularly for large amounts of data, but data entry is very time-consuming. Analysis must above all be practical. For the purposes of this discussion, we assume that as community practitioners you are unlikely to have vast data samples at your disposal, and that analysis is possible using simple tools such as coloured pencils and a passion to find an authentic meaning. Using coloured pencils is, in our opinion, an invaluable way of comparing interviews, as they enable you to track words, concepts or ideas that appear across transcripts, as well as marking process consistencies and differences, and distinguishing between negative and positive opinions. You can interpret the data and make notes in your reflective diary at the same time. You can use the same method for marking focus group transcripts, highlighting views that converge and diverge, as well as positive and negative opinions.

As discussed in Chapter 2, interpretation involves hermeneutics, or making meaning of our findings from the context in which they occur. As practitioners, when we seek to show the impact of an intervention, we are unlikely to do so without discussing the social context in which it has taken place. In the context of a job-seeking skills programme, for example, we would refer to the frequency of unemployment in the area, probably by sex and by age. Interpretation of findings is also important in terms of ideas. In our work on learning as transformation, for example, we are unlikely to discuss change without considering identity and change in identity from the perspective of the individual concerned, but we would also discuss meaning in terms of the audience for our work, as discussed in Chapter 4. One audience for the work will, of course, be the participants in the interviews, and if you are embarrassed about showing them your findings, you should consider how authentic your work is and whether you have treated the participants' points of view with neutral respect.

The use of quotations is useful for illustrative purposes, and is good practice, as it represents what people really said. However, there is a fine balance to be struck between overegging the pudding and distancing yourself too much from the words of the participants. As practitioners, we always enjoy reading the words of participants where these communicate a point well, but they can be boring if they are just listed without discussion.

You may wish to know personal details about your interviewees or focus group participants, but it is important to avoid asking some things directly in a focus group. Age is sensitive, for example, for some people, so collect this information outside of a focus group or interview situation. Similarly, care is needed in interviews when addressing deep and complex matters such as gender identity. Avoid asking too many direct demographic questions, as such information will probably emerge during the course of the interview; if not, you can always ask for outstanding details at the end. Always start with preparatory questions, and if you feel uncomfortable with the subject matter, ask yourself why you are asking the question and whether you would feel comfortable answering it. A final word goes to focus groups primarily but also applies to interviews. You may find it helpful to use activities, which can be as simple as showing a picture to stimulate discussion, or more complex, such as filling in an inventory to help people formulate their opinions, taking care to ensure not to ask leading questions or exclude items from discussion.

Interviews and focus groups can be fun, and are exciting ways of finding out about impact. They can also be very illuminating of people's experiences of your community work. As with all the methods we have discussed, reflexivity (see Chapter 2) is important – perhaps more so in the context of interviews and focus groups, as not only are you the lens for the information you generate, but you are also the tool that makes the information possible, so using a diary to record your own feelings, thoughts and ideas is particularly important. Be prepared, as suggested earlier, to be interviewed with the questions you intend to ask others, so that you can assess the impact the questions will have, as well as sequence and quality of what you are asking. Also be prepared to pilot the interview schedule or focus group schedule with others. This will provide you with feedback and enable you to assess overall quality. Interviews and focus groups provide the qualitative information that can be used to illustrate data gathered via management information systems, as discussed in Chapter 13.

Challenge questions:

1. When would you choose to conduct interviews?
2. How would you answer the interview questions that you ask others?
3. When would you choose to run a focus group?
4. How would you manage challenging individuals, such as the attention seeker or the non-participant?

Reference

Krueger, R.A. and Casey, M.A. (2009) *Focus Groups: A Practical Guide for Applied Research* (4th edn), Thousand Oaks, CA: Sage.

9

Narrative inquiry

Karen McArdle

Introduction

Narrative inquiry is a method of finding the stories we wish to tell others about the impact of the work we do in the community. It is relevant to community work, because the method is highly accessible to the respondents. It seeks deep and rich accounts of experience and is consistent with the values of community work, in that it seeks to assist participants to frame their experience rather than asking them interview questions. It is the study of the stories people tell about their lives. Its purpose is to see how participants in interview impose order on the flow of experience to make sense of events and actions in their lives (Riessman, 1993). People in general, in our experience, like to tell stories about their lives. People's stories tell us about their identity, who they are and who they have become through experience. Narratives are case studies in the context of gathering evidence.

The reason narrative inquiry is so consistent with the values of the community work profession is that it does not lead the participant in terms of what to think about or consider. In interviews, you can ask about confidence and self-esteem, but this may not be of interest to respondents, nor may they conceptualise in this way. In narrative inquiry, participants choose what to discuss and you can interpret what they say to answer your questions.

Truth

There is, however, a big question about the truth of what they say. Stories are representations of what people want to communicate, including the identity they wish to portray, as well as the impact they wish to have on the listener. I could tell you a story about the time I fell off my horse and had a traumatic brain injury that put me out of action for a good five years. At the time of telling in the first year, I would have emphasised the pain and distress this caused me and the fear I experienced. Now, ten years after the event, I will tell you about how it sparked a sense of resilience in me, which makes me able to cope really well with any other form of illness, such as the pneumonia I picked up on holiday in Peru. Both stories are true, but time has given me the ability to reflect on events, so the stories are different.

We do not generally relate experience unprocessed. We describe setting, plot and any impediments to the plot, and sometimes its meaning to us. There is an inevitable gap between my experience and my telling of it. I may also change the story depending on who is listening to it. For a doctor, I would emphasise the physical and cognitive impairment I suffered. I am also creating an image of myself in the story and I may not want some people to know about the brain trauma I experienced, as they may make what I consider false assumptions about my current cognitive abilities.

My opinion is that we cannot know the exact truth of any communication, be it in interview and narrative alike, but, in community work, which emphasises relationships, we are well placed to make professional judgements about what a person is seeking to portray through our observation of their disposition and through active listening to what is being presented.

Forms of telling

Narratives not only tell us about past experience, but also about meaning or how the individual understands this experience. The narrative may be archetypal, such as a comedy tragedy, history or romance, for example.

It may also be affected by who is listening. I once met a community worker who was male and had worked with female young victims of domestic abuse and found this worthwhile but challenging. He considered his gender had affected engagement with the young women initially; but with perseverance he was able to overcome their suspicion and work to support them well. It mattered to the young women who were listening. Similarly, we need to consider what impact a narrative interview has on the story being told. Stories may be constructed in a rather formulaic way.

It has been suggested that stories have certain elements, usually told in the following set sequence:

- an abstract (a summary of what is intended or what will follow);
- orientation (context, place, time and so on);
- complicating action (what happened and what, if anything, went wrong);
- evaluation (what it meant to the storyteller);
- resolution (what finally happened);
- coda (the moral of the tale or the perspective now) (derived from Labov and Walestsky, 1997).

In my experience, stories often embrace these elements. It is helpful to look out for them to assist with ascribing meaning, but they do not always follow this structure.

How to conduct narrative inquiry

One of the advantages of narrative inquiry is that the interview is framed not by the inquirer, but by the participants. This means that the questions asked need simply be an invitation to tell the story of an experience and to keep the story going. For the inquirer, the best starting point is often to ask, "Can you tell me about the first time you heard about the project?". The story will begin and can be followed up with probing questions such as: "What happened next?", "Can you give an example?", "How did you feel?", "Did everyone feel the same?". The key point is that you are not introducing themes for discussion. It is important to be aware, however, that although you do not find the narratives, you participate in their creation because of who you are and how you behave. You jointly construct narrative and meaning with the participant. The goal in narrative interviewing is to generate detailed accounts rather than brief answers (Riessman, 2008).

You run the risk, of course, of your participants digressing from the experience in which you are interested. This is fine and should be tolerated as much as possible, but you can choose to bring them back to the point simply by reminding them of the starting point of the discussion (the project in question), and asking them to return to it. You should be aware, however, that this involves you controlling the conversation and interrupting the participant's natural train of thought, which is why digression should be indulged as much as possible. Besides, participants will often correct themselves by saying something along the lines of "Where were we, then?".

All of this assumes that the people you are with will tell you a story. We have already discussed engaging with participants for interview (Chapter 8) and the same applies to narrative interviews. Clearly, if you know the participants, you will already have engaged with them, and just need to make sure. If you do not know the participants, you should spend some time engaging with them first. Narrative works well with children, who often very much enjoy sharing stories of their lives. Young people may be difficult to persuade to participate, so you may need to spend some time discussing their interests to break the ice and encourage them to open up and tell you a story about their experience. Participants sometimes stick rigidly to the facts, and this can be frustrating. In such cases, you will need recourse to your probing questions to elicit feeling and examples.

Interviews in narrative inquiry vary in length. When used for assessing the impact of a programme, they may last for at least an hour, often longer, as people often welcome an opportunity to share their life experiences. If you are working with children, or with learners with a language other than your own, and are unsure of how well they will respond, you can stimulate discussion by encouraging the participant to create a visual representation of an experience. Riessman (2008) proposes three sites of visual analysis, summarised as follows:

- the image-making process;
- the image itself;
- the reaction of the audience to the image.

Ethics

Ethics is particularly important for narrative inquiry, which is usually a rich and deep form of scrutiny, and may be emotive for the individual doing the telling. Ethics is discussed in the context of interviews in Chapter 8, and all this applies to narrative inquiry, but it is particularly important in this context to remember to renegotiate consent throughout the duration of the story. This simply means repeating questions such as "Are you happy to go on?" and "Do you want to stop now?". Clearly if a person looks distressed, you would stop immediately, take off your inquiring hat, put on your other professional hat and either seek support or help the individual yourself, depending on your qualifications and skills.

People sometimes find themselves revealing more than they intended in telling stories about their lives and feelings. It is important to be sensitive to this and make an ethical judgement about whether talking is therapeutic and cathartic, or, at worst, insidious and undermining. If in doubt, you should stop the interview and support the participant.

Data analysis

Data analysis is always important, but in narrative inquiry it is crucial to helping to understand what we have been told. The first decision to make is whether to transcribe the narrative. Clearly it is best to do so and is crucial in research, but if you are unable or do not have the time, it is important to listen to the story or stories repeatedly, and, we suggest, at least transcribe the elements that seem significant to you. One of the features of narrative inquiry is that when you use quotations in a presentation to illustrate a point, it generally takes longer than usual to convey a sense of the meaning of a whole story. Narrative inquiry seeks to capture the whole story rather than reducing it to small elements.

Data analysis involves looking at the whole story and seeing what purpose was in the mind of the narrator. Riessman (2008) discusses persuasiveness, which she links to plausibility. Is the story reasonable and convincing? Is it coherent with themes reflecting other themes so that there is consistency? Rather than looking at themes, we look at each holistic case. This does not mean we cannot compare cases, as long as we are aware that it is difficult and unrealistic to compare people and their detailed accounts to each other. We can compare opinions about programmes.

If you transcribe, you will be analysing as you do so. The first thing to think about is the structure of the story rather than the content. Why does the participant tell their story in this way rather than any other way? What does the nature of your relationship with the participant tell you about how they have told the story? You may wish to compare the participant's view of reality with your own to see where there are similarities and differences. Content analysis or thematic analysis requires careful study of the text and identification of themes that recur or are significant to the narrative. You are assessing what is said. Often it is helpful to look at how things are said, the metaphors used and the images that are represented or the examples used to illustrate points.

You will need to interpret narrative, especially in cases where participants are unused to using conceptual ideas such as confidence or self-esteem. For example, the following extract from a recovering drug user suggests confidence but does not use this word:

> 'I found the yoga exercises really great, they made me stronger and I was able to go and use the drug centre with this ... this kind of quietness. Before I was scared to go.' (Jill)

Similarly, self-esteem can be deduced from this story by a young person on an employability programme, even if the word itself is not used:

'I never saw the point in getting up. I had nothing I wanted to do. I just lay there or slept…. It was fine. Then I decided I wanted to do something. I don't know what yet but I do. I want to make the best I can 'cause I'm worth it. You know like they say in that ad [advert].' (John)

Narrative analysis requires interpreting what is said and the best way to do this is to illustrate what is said with an example. I did a narrative analysis with learners on a programme called Reach Out, funded with an employability agenda that seeks to work with individuals before they start looking for a job. Participants included ex-offenders, those recovering from alcohol or drug misuse, and people with mental health issues. I reflected on the interviews and read the transcripts of participants talking about their experiences of the programme. After conceptualising what had been said, my analysis found that the programme had had an impact on identity, learning, wellbeing and social presence. There was also evidence of longitudinal impact. Each of these is examined in more detail in the following sections.

Identity

Identity is not just something that we are; it is something we construct and actively live by (Holstein and Gubrium, 2000). Experience provides the means by which one becomes conscious of who one is. Self is also a social idea in that we have different personas with different people. The purpose behind this description of the author's understanding of identity is that identity change is fundamental to the Reach Out programme.

   Identity was important in the evaluation of the programme, as respondents indicated change and transition from a point of social isolation or negative behaviour before engaging with Reach Out to an identity of participation in a learning community and its activities afterwards. There are benefits to both the individual and wider society from the former's positive experiences of participation in a community context. Put simply, participants saw themselves differently after contact with Reach Out, not only in terms of perception of self, but also in positive behaviours.

The following are examples of quotations that led in part to this conceptualisation of the findings:

'Over the years I've come out mair and mair [more and more] and here it's totally Reach Out. Especially drink … on the proper road … I'm meeting great folk, similar lifestyles, ken [you know].' (Alastair)

'Before I came to Reach Out I had isolated myself from my friends. Had difficulty getting up in the morning. I was heavily medicated and had been like that for a while. I spent all 2012 in hospital. I come here and do things and it makes a difference to my days, my weeks. I have to be here for 9.15 and have to get myself up in the morning. Reach Out creates a reason to get up. It's an effort to get going but I get myself here.' (Alastair)

'… I'm working now as a volunteer. R [name] asked me to do it. That's just happening. I have skills that I had forgotten about. I'm quite looking forward to it. I can see what develops and see what I am capable of.' (Jane)

'At that stage I could have gone either way ether [sic] shooting myself or ending up in prison. R [name of community worker], with guidance, made me think of my family. I'd better look before I threw it all away, ken [you know]. I've never been diagnosed with bipolar before but I get extremely depressed and it comes and goes. I get highs. I've been diagnosed with ADHD [attention deficit hyperactivity disorder]. My son he's got autism and I never notice his cues either. I've learnt to adapt in the big wide world and things. My mother spend [sic] time with my sister because she thought I was fine because I was clever and at primary school it was bad. I was always kinda judged by people but when I came here I wasn't judged.' (Jim)

Learning

Reach Out is an educational programme, but it has a holistic dimension that embraces health and wellbeing, as well as recovery from issues such as substance misuse and integration of offenders into the community. It looks at the whole person and seeks to integrate them into a nourishing community. The learning dimension is captured by Peter Jarvis's definitions of learning as transformation from one kind of being through experience into another way of being. There were overt learning experiences, new skills and knowledge, but also the learning that comes with transformation of identity and knowledge of self. Apparent was learning linked to the early steps of employment training in terms of routine and self-management, as well as more directly related employment skills such as information and communications technology skills. Learning was also apparent across the life course after contact with Reach Out, with participants reporting growth in life skills and qualities such as self-esteem, confidence and in particular social skills.

> 'Before I came here I was really closed up. Now I'm the loudest one here. Come out of my shell. I was hiding behind a mask. It was dog eat dog and I was going to do the eating. It was all just a front. Doing the football I learned to be discipline as well as control and now I can do that with the kids, take control at tea time and things. I got money, paid the bills, sorted out the problems.' (Jim)

> 'I volunteered with the class. I kind of got a confidence thing from that. They thought I could do it so I did.' (Jim)

> 'My first day I was nervous, it was the most nerve-wracking thing I had ever done to come along to Reach Out. All the people. There were ten in the IT class but now I've got a job…. Reach Out gave me something to do for the whole day. Before that

I had nothing and the people and the ... everything ... were what made Reach Out important.' (Kevin)

Wellbeing

Wellbeing is notoriously difficult to define but frequently occurs in discussion, linked to the notion of health, where health is reciprocally defined as physical, emotional and social wellbeing. Wellbeing was apparent as a transformative outcome of the Reach Out programme where quality of life improved greatly for some individuals, manifest in particular in improved confidence and self-esteem. Physical and social wellbeing also substantially improved. One individual reported a change from being an isolated, housebound alcoholic to an individual who had found a job and rode to the place of work by bike:

'I used to take panic attacks quite often and I wasn't able to sit in a room with people. I went to college and was not able to sit in the room. I told the teacher I had to go out and I could not go on a bus. Now I come down here on the bus all the time. I used to plan my routes into town so I could avoid as many people as possible but now I can get off a bus on Union Street [main street] and I still have difficulty but I have learnt a walking meditation. It's still difficult but I can do it.' (Bob)

Social presence

Social presence was identified as another benefit of the programme. Participants frequently reported social isolation prior to attending the programme, and improvement was linked to the value of social interaction with peers in the group setting. There was a sense of security derived from shared prior and ongoing experiences. Participants cited support for recovery and personal development, which in turn led to wider participation in the community as volunteers and participation in other social opportunities, indicative of a developing social presence. Individuals were testing the water of social interaction at the programme and finding that they were able to rediscover a social persona that had disappeared in times of substance misuse. This in turn benefitted the wider community as well as the wellbeing of the individual.

'I was isolated and anxious at first and I wanted to do something to get out and about. R [facilitator] is a great guy and makes you feel at home and I wanted to do walking because I had put on weight and healthy minds are important.... What I was really needing ... I can isolate myself and that's not good for me, it's really bad for me. So I was coming out and meeting people and getting out of my flat which is really important.' (Jane)

'I was struggling with mental health. I was pretty bad at that stage. I met R [name]. Lovely guy, and he gave me something to look forward to. I did dynamics and football at first and it was sociable and welcoming and I'd never experienced anything like that before.' (Rick)

Longitudinal impact

It was apparent from the research that Reach Out had often had a substantial impact, made up of small steps along a growth and development journey. Immediate and short-term outcomes, while apparent, were only part of the story. Individuals reported that they had made progress over considerable time (years rather than months) based on the Reach Out experiences they had had. Reach Out has a long-term and sustainable impact on people's lives. To expect that challenged individuals would enter the workforce immediately is unrealistic, for example, but some of the most troubled individuals begin on a path that will ultimately lead to social integration and indeed perhaps a job or further study. This has implications for the funding outcomes for Reach Out, which should recognise the long-term transitions that are required for some individuals from a highly troubled life to integrate fully into the community and workforce. Funding should take into account the social return on investment of the programme, with savings in particular to budgets linked to rehabilitation of offenders, social work budgets and budgets linked to mental and physical health and wellbeing.

> 'I've been coming for five or six years now. I drop in sometimes. I'm working just now but quit my job yesterday because I need more time for paternity. R is great for guidance on all things. He doesn't give advice just guidance like. It holds me together. Stress levels are crazy just now because I need a job but need to be there for the family. There may be a job in the air the noo [now].' (Jim)

It is hoped that the example of Reach Out has helped you to think about analysis of the stories people tell you. It is often what we see behind the words that is the most important dimension of what is said.

Challenge questions

1. How do you think you would influence storytellers by your gender identity, ethnicity and cultural background?
2. What stories do you tell of your life to others and why?
3. How can you make sure that your outcomes are covered in a narrative without distorting the story with your questions?

References

Holstein J.F. and Gubrium, J.F. (2000) *The Self we Live By: Narrative Identity in a Postmodern World*, Oxford: Oxford University Press.

Labov, W., and Walestsky, J. (1997) Narrative analysis: Oral versions of personal experience, *Journal of Narrative Life History*, 3–38.

Riessman, C. (1993) *Narrative Analysis*, Newbury Park, CA: Sage.

Riessman, C. (2008) *Narrative Methods for the Human Sciences*, Thousand Oaks, CA: Sage.

10

Collaborative and participatory approaches

Karen McArdle

Introduction

> Ultimately, participatory research is about respecting
> and understanding the people with whom researchers
> work. It is about developing a realization that local
> people are knowledgeable and that they, together
> with researchers, can work towards analyses and
> solutions. It involves recognizing the rights of those
> whom research concerns, enabling people to set their
> own agendas for research and development and so
> giving them ownership over the process. (Cornwall
> and Jewkes, 1995: 1675)

This quotation refers to the importance of respecting the people
with whom we work and affirms that local people can work in
a research or, we would say, evidence gathering, context. It also
affirms the rights of these participants to set their own agendas
for inquiry and to have ownership of the process. Participatory
approaches can also be viewed from a more pragmatic
perspective. The following quotation enumerates some of the
practical advantages of participatory research.

> [Participatory research] raises the likelihood that
> research questions and designs will be more responsive
> to community needs; that research executions will

be more accurate in capturing community nuances; and that community members, having been brought into the research enterprise, will be more likely to pay attention to, agree with, and implement the recommendations of the research findings. (Jason, 2006, p xvii)

Approaches to gathering evidence that involve working together with participants are sometimes called collaborative approaches, and sometimes participatory approaches. Collaborative approaches typically involve communities of practice with different stakeholders functioning as co-inquirers (Messiou, 2019). Participatory approaches typically involve the clients, learners or service users. They are founded on the fundamental principle that most people can and will participate in the generation of evidence in a research-focused environment. Those who see research as an elitist and difficult activity find this approach hard to comprehend, but we are of the view that, with appropriate training and support, most people are well able to contribute at all stages of a research, inquiry and/ or evidence-gathering activity should they choose to do so. It is important to accept this principle, if we genuinely believe in equality and inclusion. The following case study is an example of successful collaboration.

A local health network, made up of professionals in the fields of health and social care in a rural community in Scotland, came together to discuss why some local people did not access the health and wellbeing services provided. They decided they needed to collaborate to do research, but were not sure how to proceed. So they decided to employ an academic from the local university to help them with the research and with some training. This worked well, as it brought together local knowledge and more theoretical knowledge about inquiry and the social issues faced in the wider community. The research project uncovered a culture of fear of outsiders and of new incomers to the local community, which meant traditional residents preferred to stay away from new initiatives. Accordingly, members of the network knew that they had work to do to break down, through community development, these fears and suspicions about people coming in from outside. It was a very good collaboration between health professionals from a range of disciplines and the university.

There is a strong tradition of participatory approaches to research in education, health and community contexts, where value is placed on participation. Increasingly, public participation is being sought on government policy in these and other areas. Some argue that this is a result of declining confidence in the processes that develop public policy; others see it as an inevitable extension of increasing access to information and democratic processes. One strong reason for participation is seen, for example, in the field of health, where this form of inquiry seeks to include people in vulnerable health situations. Such collaborations enable collective action to improve local situations, as well as to reduce structural inequalities and health disparities (Groot et al, 2019).

Participatory approaches have a long tradition and a strong credibility in the research field, having gained popularity in the 1970s and 1980s and now being frequently linked to an action research process, described later in this chapter. Participatory approaches are linked to the values we hold about the rights of our participants and the relationship we consider to be appropriate with our participants. This is inevitably linked to our notions of power and the power that we consider appropriate and are prepared to accord to our participants in our profession. The authors of this text consider that, if we live in a democracy, power should be distributed as much as possible and, accordingly, participatory approaches are inherently desirable.

The extract from Jason (2006) quoted earlier refers to the increased accuracy we can anticipate from using a participatory approach, and this is again a question of the power we hold as professionals. We need to ask ourselves if we can truly 'know' what the impact has been of what we have done. Are we asking the right questions? Or have we framed the question from our professional perspective? It is very easy to design an instrument to gather evidence, such as a questionnaire or interview schedule, that will find out what you want to know about a project, but you have to question whether you want to know the right things. Framing an interview schedule on your own will tell you whether the impact has been in the regions that you think it has been. Framing an interview schedule with participants will tell you what they think it is important that you know. This framing is a vital theme in the gathering of evidence. Practitioners must be sure they are asking the right questions, not the questions they want to ask or the usual questions derived from a template.

The two main negatives of using participatory approaches are that they are time-consuming and they demand developed skills of engagement. The time factor is needed because the practitioner needs to assist participants and induct them in an accessible way into the processes of gathering of evidence. This demands an ability to engage participants to be interested, as well as an ability to provide training at an appropriate level to decide what to explore, to design a method, to ask the right questions and to analyse and create meaning from what is gathered. We return to these processes later in this chapter. Suffice it to say that we consider participatory approaches to be worth the effort and worth the sacrifice of the polished professional voice in favour of more authentic evidence in the voice of participants.

Children, young people and vulnerable adults

The emphasis on the importance of listening to the voices of children, young people and vulnerable adults has increased substantially over the past two decades, including of children in an early childhood setting (Harcourt and Einarsdottir, 2011). In the latter case, this is because of changes in the way childhood is viewed. Children are now regarded as 'beings' rather than 'becomings', and hence are seen as worthy of investigation in their own right (Harcourt and Einarsdottir, 2011). With regard to children, young people and vulnerable adults, it is necessary to avoid the dichotomy of thinking that these populations are either vulnerable and dependent, or invulnerable and competent, as both are probably true for most people. It is also important to remember there is a co-construction of reality for most people whereby reality or 'voice' is dependent on speaker and listener. Meaning is created by the listener, so two voices or multi-voices are always present. Listening and listening actively to children, young people and vulnerable adults is a starting point, but, simultaneously, we should be aware of how their lives are circumscribed, often necessarily by the action of adults.

Harcourt and Einarsdottir (2011) suggest that, when young children are treated as equals, they can take ownership and actively participate in every stage of an inquiry process. This, of course, applies to older young people and adults too. Hart's Ladder of Participation (1992) is widely known and used to conceptualise engagement with participants of all ages. The following version, derived from Halliday and colleagues (2019), shows rungs of the ladder representing levels of engagement by young people. You may wish to consider the place of your evidence gathering on these rungs and what this means. Which rungs, for example, would be listed as participation or engagement and which as non-participation?

- Rung 8: Initiated by young people; decisions made in partnership with adults.
- Rung 7: Initiated by young people; action directed by youth with little input from adults.
- Rung 6: Initiated by adults; shared decision making with youth.
- Rung 5: Adults make decisions; young people are consulted and informed.
- Rung 4: Young people are assigned tasks and informed about how and why they are involved in a project.
- Rung 3: Young people have token participation with little or no influence.
- Rung 2: Young people are used as 'decoration' to help adults' initiatives.
- Rung 1: Adults manipulate young people to support their own projects and pretend they are the result of young people's inspiration (derived from Halliday et al, 2019: 176).

In work with children, young people and adults, we need a detailed and in-depth understanding of the associated ethical principles, norms and guidelines or legal requirements. These vary by profession and country of origin, but it is crucial that key ethical ideas are managed. It is relevant here to recommend the work undertaken at Durham University (Durham Community Research Team, 2011) in the UK on ethics in participatory research in general.

Managing anonymity and confidentiality is an important and sometimes difficult process. You must be aware of any legal requirements to pass on information about child protection issues, for example. It is also important and difficult to avoid deception, for example in cases where you may wish to simplify ideas for the participants but run the risk of distorting the meaning of the inquiry. Obtaining informed consent can be difficult for similar reasons; it is essential to check that your participants have truly understood what is involved, and you must adhere to requirements to obtain parental or carer consent in the relevant circumstances.

While there are ethical requirements to which you must adhere in working with vulnerable people, the whole process of participation demands an ethical focus where 'shoulds' and 'oughts' are questioned and where an assumption is made that people 'can' and are 'able' in most cases to participate at some level and must be treated in accordance with this respectful assumption.

Inquiry as empowerment

> ... I saw a bumper sticker on a car with a quote from George Orwell: 'In a time of universal deceit, telling the truth is a revolutionary act.' It seems to me that we are always in a time of universal deceit because of the ubiquity of injustice. (Denzin and Giardina, 2010: 113)

Empowerment is a much-contested topic (Aldred, 2011). As a practitioner, I have seen it used in a local government planning context to describe tokenistic consultation with residents about decisions that have already made. This is to be avoided and is not embraced by our understanding of empowerment.

Empowerment is both a value orientation for working in the community and a theoretical model for understanding the process and consequences of efforts to exert control and influence over decisions that affect one's life (Zimmerman, 2000).

Much of the literature on participatory approaches and empowerment assumes that the inquirers have an agenda and subsequently encourage participants to join in the inquiry (McArdle, 2014). This, we suggest, is not complete empowerment. Empowerment can be more authentically embedded in the processes of community practice by enabling participants to decide if, how and when evidence should be gathered; this can be done as part of the community engagement process in community development. Community development, we argue, is predominantly a learning process in which the professional engages with a community to assist community members to come together to learn about their situation and take collective action and generate solutions to common problems. Jason and colleagues (2004) help with the connection between participation, empowerment and learning. They argue that participatory approaches to research can empower in three ways:

- through the specific insights, new understandings and new options they (participants) discover in the process of enquiring about their social reality;
- by learning from each other thus enhancing their understanding of social reality through dialogue;
- by learning how to transform their own social reality, thus turning knowledge into social praxis. (Jason et al, 2004, p 22)

Fetterman and Wandersman (2005: 2) describe the key principles of empowerment evaluation as follows:

- improvement
- community ownership
- inclusion
- democratic participation
- social justice
- community knowledge

- evidence-based strategies
- capacity building
- organisational learning
- accountability

We choose to discuss two of these principles together: accountability and social justice. Accountability is crucial. To whom do we wish to be accountable? Is it our funders? Is it our stakeholders, or is it our supervisor or boss? Fundamentally, surely, it should be our participants, if we offer them a service they are in a position to choose to use, as opposed to it being a mandatory statutory service. We also consider it important to acknowledge the place of social justice in empowerment, as indicated by Fetterman and Wandersman (2005), as it is linked to gathering evidence. Ledwith (2016) in discussing social justice, calls on us to 'understand the ways in which structural discrimination is sewn into society, resulting in inequalities that lead to social marginalisation and exclusion' (p 11).

Denzin and Giardina (2010) argue that the conclusion of qualitative research communicated in ways that combine advocacy with accuracy can counter the promotion of 'structured deceit': '… – that is the deliberate and nondeliberate covering up of the truth about how particular sets of people actually live their lives' (p 11).

It is important to be aware that research access and processes, and, therefore, inquiry access and processes, can be marginalising and excluding in many ways, not least in terms of presentation of findings. Ledwith (2016) describes how Freire, in his seminal work *Pedagogy of the Oppressed* (1972), challenged the dominant assumptions of traditional research by asking, '(a) whose ideas are informing the research questions and in whose interests is it taking place, (b) who is controlling the research process, and (c) who decides on the results and outcomes of the research for whose benefit? (Ledwith, 2016, p 146). These questions take to a new level the issues linked to accountability and power dynamics mentioned earlier in this chapter. To summarise, there is a complex interlinking of the ideas of accountability, empowerment and social justice that lead us to value highly participatory approaches to gathering evidence. For some, a sufficient level of participation is considered to be focus groups and surveys, or representation on an advisory committee (Rowe and Frewer, 2004). We consider this to be inadequate.

Participatory action research

Participatory action research (PAR) is defined in many different ways, but the underpinning principles are that it is a systematic approach to collective investigation by the people that the questions or problems concern. It blends the strengths of professional practitioners with the lived experience of participants. 'It explicitly works for change and so has an intrinsically critical edge with the potential for addressing directly issue of power and equity in working to make things better' (Denzin and Giardina, 2010: 117).

Referring to young people in school, Halliday and colleagues enumerate some of the advantages of PAR to participants:

> Studies suggest that PAR improves communication skills, problem solving, critical thinking, self efficacy, confidence, self regulatory capacity, public speaking, research skills, overall well being, and helps participants to be better students. (Halliday et al, 2019: 177)

In the next section, we discuss the practical ways in which you may include participants in the evidence-gathering process.

There are many books on PAR and action research, and it is a process of action and reflection in cycles of inquiry. It is very well suited to the processes of inquiry associated with community work as appropriate for working with complex questions, with participants, and with a focus on change. Here, we focus on the participatory dimension of this and other approaches to inquiry.

Establishing the focus of the inquiry

It is often the case that we have an inquiry focus in mind and choose to engage participants in the process. It is important too to think about how we might engage participants in deciding exactly what the inquiry will be about. We may have in mind a research project, but the participants would prefer a consultation or perhaps no inquiry at all. This overlaps with engaging participants in the process, as they may find inquiry intimidating and choose not to engage for this reason. You may need to emphasise the excitement and interest inherent in evidence gathering, and reassure the participants that they are capable of doing it and that you will provide the necessary training and support.

Training and support

Training and support on how to undertake an inquiry and gather evidence may well be very important. If your evidence is to be trustworthy and robust, the process must also be trustworthy and robust. There is no point in a participatory focus if the inquiry is to be second-class. This does participants a disservice when they deserve better if they choose to participate.

Training should focus on choices and the advantages and disadvantages of the different approaches to inquiry. You should consider 'power' and its relevance to choices about the inquiry approach. Participants should understand that the continuation of a project may be dependent on numerical data, or perhaps statistics and stories, if this is the case. Participants in my experience are inclined to prefer surveys for inquiries, as this is what they know and recognise, but you should give them choice to enable them to determine the most appropriate method.

Implementation

It is important to frame inquiry as achievable and accessible. Once the process has been chosen, support is essential to help participants with its implementation, which means providing training in interviewing, group dynamics or whichever skills are relevant to the inquiry. In running a focus group, for example, it may help to couple participants with a more skilled person to ensure the quality of discussion.

Ethics

The most important aspect of training for participants is learning about appropriate behaviour and how to manage ethics. Participants must be aware of the requirements of informed consent and the right to withdraw, as well as how to avoid deception, how to guarantee confidentiality/anonymity, and how to behave in a way that is research-minded or respectful.

Analysis and interpretation

Analysis and interpretation should be led by the practitioner, as the skills required arguably take some time to acquire, but participation in this activity is still desirable, as ascribing meaning to what is found out allows participants to supply local and personal meanings to data and evidence. Brydon-Miller and Coghlan (2019: 309) provide a useful description of dialogues that will help with developing shared meanings:

> The mode of dialogue that is marked by suspending one's own presuppositions and engaging in internal listening, inquiring, accepting difference and building mutual trust, revealing feelings, building common ground and challenging one's own assumptions and learning to think and feel in order that the whole group may build new and shared assumptions and meanings.

We should aim for robustness and validity in the inquiry we conduct with participants. Denzin and Giardina (2010: 85) provide helpful guidance on validity and its relationship to participation, implicit in ideas of emancipation, empowerment and advancement of human rights:

> Today it seems that epistemic criteria concerned with truth, reliability, validity and simplicity in inquiry are increasingly replaced by ethical and political criteria that emphasize emancipation, empowerment, care, solidarity, and the advancement of human rights as generative aims of social research activities.

Reporting

Participants will need support if they are not used to writing reports or giving talks, but this does not mean they should not do so. Finding accessible ways of reporting is important, perhaps through the use of a leaflet, with images selected by participants. Reporting is discussed in more detail in Chapter 4. The following case study provides an example of initiating a successful participatory research project.

> Anuja organised a participatory research project in a run-down, rural town in Scotland to find out what the needs of the local community were in terms of community projects that would assist with generating community spirit. The local committee formed to run the project consisted of members of local associations and clubs. When Anuja asked what they wished to do, they were quite clear that they wanted to produce a questionnaire, as this would influence the local council more than any other form of research. Anuja explained other options to them, as she was worried about issues of literacy and accessibility, but they were quite clear about their preference, so a questionnaire was what they did. Convinced by some of Anuja's arguments, they decided to make the questionnaire available online for young people and to use structured interviews for those who might find it difficult to complete, such as elderly folk. They organised a family fun day to bring people together to complete the questionnaire. The final results of the questionnaire, which had been completed by 76% of the population, were presented by the residents to the local council. The council subsequently agreed to act on the local community's desires, including, most importantly, to erect a Christmas tree, which was intended to – and did, according to the residents – promote feelings of wellbeing and community spirit in the town.

The final word goes to Denzin and Giardina (2010), who argue that rights are crucial to the practice of social research, and that if we do not include participants in an inquiry about them, we should be able to justify why this is the case. Only if the process were disempowering or harmful would there be any reason to exclude them.

> It is impossible to understand the acts of a parent, a teacher, or a police officer without taking into account the positions and storylines that bring meaning to their activities. Social processes are therefore saturated with rights, negotiations of rights and, alas, violations of rights. Consequently, my point is that an understanding of rights should not be a separate pastime activity, which the morally committed social analyst may engage in from time to time, for social life is epistemically inconceivable if stripped of the normativities generated by rights and duties. All social research thus needs an awareness of rights. (Denzin and Giardina, 2010: 94).

Challenge questions

1. Do you like the people you work with; if so, why, and if not, why not?
2. Could you work collaboratively with these people? What is making you say yes or what is stopping you?
3. Do you believe in equality and inclusion? If so, why not be participatory?
4. How would you engage your participants to collaborate? If you think they would not be willing, why is this the case?

References

Aldred, R. (2011) From community participation to organizational therapy? World Café and Appreciative Inquiry as research methods, *Community Development Journal*, 46(1): 57–71.

Brydon-Miller, M. and Coghlan, B. (2019) First-, second- and third-person values-based ethics in educational action research: personal resonance, mutual regard and social responsibility, *Educational Action Research*, 27(2): 318–30.

Cornwall, A. and Jewkes, R. (1995) What is participatory research?, *Social Science & Medicine*, 41(12): 1667–76.

Denzin, N.K. and Giardina, M.D. (2010) *Qualitative Inquiry and Human Rights*, Walnut Creek, CA: Left Coast Press.

Durham Community Research Team (2011) *Community-Based Participatory Research: Ethical Challenges*, Durham: Centre for Social Justice and Community Action, Durham University, available at: https://ahrc.ukri.org/documents/project-reports-and-reviews/connected-communities/community-based-participatory-research-ethical-challenges

Fetterman, D.M. and Wandersman, A. (2005) *Empowerment Evaluation: Principles in Practice*, New York, NY: Guilford Press.

Freire, P. (1972) *Pedagogy of the Oppressed*, Harmondsworth: Penguin.

Groot, B.C., Vink, M., Haveman, A., Huberts, M., Schout, G. and Abma, T.A. (2019) Ethics of care in participatory health research: mutual responsibility in collaboration with co-researchers, *Educational Action Research*, 27(2): 286–302.

Halliday, A.J., Kern, M.J., Garrett, D.K. and Turnbull, D.A. (2019) The student voice in well being: a case study of participatory action research in positive education, *Educational Action Research*, 27(2): 173–96.

Harcourt, D. and Einarsdottir, J. (2011) Introducing children's perspectives and participation in research, *European Early Childhood Education Research Journal*, 19(3): 301–7.

Hart, R. (1992) *Children's Participation: From Tokenism to Citizenship*, Florence: UNICEF Innocenti Research Centre.

Jason, L. (2006) Benefits and challenges of generating community participation, *Professional Psychology: Research and Practice*, 37(2): 132.

Jason, L., Keys, C., Suarez-Balcazar, Y., Taylor, R. and Davis, M. (2004) *Participatory Community Research: Theories and Methods in Action*, Washington, DC: American Psychological Association.

Ledwith, M. (2016) *Community Development in Action: Putting Freire into Practice*, Bristol: Policy Press.

McArdle, K. (2014) 'Research as empowerment: blending PAR with community development', in T. Stern, A. Townsend, F. Rauch and A. Schuster (eds) *Action Research, Innovation and Change: International Perspectives across Disciplines*, New York, NY: Routledge: 73–88.

Messiou, K. (2019) Collaborative action research: facilitating inclusion is schools, *Educational Action Research*, 27(2): 197–209.

Rowe, G. and Frewer, J. (2004) Evaluating public-participation exercises: a research agenda, *Science, Technology and Human Values*, 29(4): 512–56.

Zimmerman, M.A. (2000) 'Empowerment theory', in J. Rappaport and E. Seidman (eds) *Handbook of Community Psychology*, Boston, MA: Springer, pp 43–63.

11

Social impact studies

Ed Garrett

'We need to stop investing in activities that don't make a difference and start investing in activities that do.' (Social return on investment consultant)

Introduction

Showing evidence of social impact is nothing new for those working in and with communities; the social is what we have always been interested in. However, the process and profile of this way of showing evidence has changed in recent years. Expectations of corporate social responsibility on the private sector, to demonstrate its social as well as its financial value, through some process of social impact measurement, have translated to demands from funders, investors and commissioners for more robust ways of capturing social impact, from those working in the public and third sectors (Arvidson and Lyon, 2014). The measurement of social impact therefore has become closely associated with approaches such as social accounting and social return on investment, which have this apparent rigour. Although such approaches can be valuable, there are other ways of showing evidence of social impact that may be more familiar to practitioners working in the community.

Some definitions

Before going on to consider some of these approaches, let us make clearer what social impact measurement involves. First, of course, it considers impact. As the introduction to this book explains, impact is about change and, more specifically, it is about the effects of the activity that brings about this change. This understanding suggests a clear link of attribution between the activity and the impact. However, this understanding does not seem to be universally used and the distinction between impacts and outcomes in particular seems to be a matter of debate (or more likely confusion) (Maas, 2009). There is no need to be too worried about this and certainly no need to get bogged down in trying to establish common understandings. You should just be aware that certain funders, commissioners and others may have varied understandings of the term impact.

Second, stakeholders consider the social dimension of impact. The social here means not only groups and communities but also individuals. It may not be immediately obvious what social value is, and this contested nature is important, as this chapter goes on to show. At the very least, however, social value can be contrasted with financial value, the dominant form of value within a market-driven viewpoint.

Third, stakeholders usually attempt to provide some way of measuring this social impact. As Maas (2009) suggests, measurement of social value is difficult and this difficulty has led to the development of many different measurement tools. For example, it is much easier to measure the numbers of people coming to a group than the impact of the group on these people. However, it is also much less interesting. Measurement is at least about providing a common frame of reference that can allow for comparison. Social return on investment studies are an attempt to do this by giving the social value a financial value. Other approaches are not so ambitious, but do involve attempts to measure impact in a way that makes sense. This issue of measurement is a tricky one and we return to it later in this chapter.

Reasons to use these approaches

There is undoubtedly a tension in the reasons for using social impact measurement, particularly for those in the third sector. Pressure to demonstrate social impact most often comes from funders. Arvidson and Lyon (2014) argue that it is part of a process of control by funders over organisations working with a social purpose. The increased emphasis on auditing and value for money is a way of consolidating the differences in power between the funders and the funded. It can squeeze out the innovative and the local, particularly if the funder decides the exact nature of the social value. So, the obvious reason for wishing to evidence social impact is really rather a negative one: social impact is what funders, commissioners and management are often most interested in.

Although this is a necessary starting point for any practitioner, there are lots of other, more positive, reasons for providing evidence of social impact. Fundamentally we are also interested in our own social impact; it is what we are about, as the following case study suggests.

> Some of us have been involved in projects that have supported refugees coming to Scotland. Because these projects are funded from a central source, it is easy to work out the financial impact of some of our interventions. For example, Mohammad was supported by adult learning and employability workers to learn English and apply for a job. When he moved into employment, we could calculate the savings, as he no longer received housing benefit or unemployment benefits, he no longer attended language classes, nor did he need specialist employability support or use of the Arabic speaking support service. We know the date of his arrival and so we can calculate the costs of the various interventions he received until he gained employment. Having supported him into employment, we can confidently attribute his success to the adult learning and employability support he received.

But while we can measure the financial return on our investment, some of the social returns are, perhaps, harder to understand. For example, we heard that, as one of the first refugees in the area to move into employment, he and his family were treated with more respect within his community, and when he attended the mosque. And although we know that, as his language skills improved rapidly in employment, he no longer required a translator for straightforward health or dental appointments, it is hard to measure the impact this had on his self-esteem and confidence without further evaluation.

Social impact studies allow for the exploration of the extent and type of change brought about by a particular intervention or funding investment. To this extent, they show if this intervention has worked, and, importantly, whether it is worth investing in again and how it can be made sustainable. Social impact studies contribute to our learning as practitioners and inform the direction of the organisations for whom we work. They also allow for the possibility of comparisons between interventions and the learning and improvement that can come from these comparisons. These considerations are as important for the practitioner as they are for the funder, commissioner or manager. We all want to know whether what we have done has brought about the change we thought it might, and what this change looks like. We want to be able to compare with other bits of work we have done or similar projects elsewhere and learn what has worked well and what could be improved.

There are other, more practical, reasons for choosing this approach. As we explore in a later section, there is a range of different tools that are suited to different kinds of project. These tools allow for the capturing of impact at a range of levels, whether that be individual, community or broader social impact. They can also be matched to the capacity and resources of organisations; some are relatively easy to use and do not involve a great deal of time and new skills on behalf of those using them; others, such as social accounting, may take greater investment but are more robust. Like all approaches to evidencing impact in community work, there is a balance to be sought between time spent gathering evidence and time spent creating impact. The important thing to do is to recognise that they support each other. If you can use participatory approaches to improve this process of mutual support, so much the better.

Finally as Arvidson and Lyon's research (2014) shows, many social purpose organisations have in fact used the requirements for social impact measurement as spaces of resistance, using the results of these evaluations to promote the value of their own organisation as well as to report to funders and commissioners. They are a good advertising tool.

Theory underpinning social impact studies

Before looking in detail at some examples of social impact approaches and case studies of how they have worked in practice, it is worth dwelling a little bit on some of the theory that underpins these approaches. This theory is not of mere academic interest. Theory lies at the centre of social impact studies. Also, as argued in Chapter 1, theory exists in a dynamic relationship with practice in which they both constantly inform each other. Without some theoretical understandings, we become what Freire called 'mere activists'; we don't really learn.

Although we need to be critically aware of an evaluation culture that may seek to control social outcomes, there is also radical potential in this approach when we consider it from a theoretical perspective. Marx provides a useful distinction on value here. He argued that a capitalist economy is dominated by exchange value, the value of a good in relation to its worth in terms of the unit of exchange, or money. This is to be distinguished from use value, the value of something in direct relation to the person who has that good (Marx, 1990). For example, the value of an intervention in community work, such as a befriending service, has a different value to the funder or commissioner, who will at least be looking for best value in terms of money, from the person benefitting from the service who will emphasise the social contact. By breaking the apparently self-evident link between money and value, social impact studies are part of an opening of an understanding of social justice in which other goods need to be promoted.

There is also a deeper point about how we know things, or epistemology, here. To promote these goods, we need to know what they are. However, exactly what constitutes social value is not immediately obvious, apart from its contrast to financial or environmental value. Different people will have different ideas. So, to return to our example of the befriending service, the person receiving the service may value the social contact, carers may value the respite and the volunteer may value the experience as a step towards employment. To build up an understanding of social value, we must capture this range of voices. There is no one understanding of social value. Knowledge of it is built up by those who contribute to this process rather than there being some expert view. Knowledge, then, is participatory and shifting, and being constantly negotiated rather than imposed by some professional. This is exciting, but also challenging.

Besides these points about social justice and knowledge, there is another way in which theory is crucial to understanding social impact approaches. Let us start by revisiting one of the examples given at the beginning of Chapter 1, that of Ryan and the groups for people who have been recently bereaved. He wants to demonstrate the value of the groups, although there is often significant drop-off in attendance during the time of the group meeting. Taking a social impact approach, Ryan will want to understand the social value of attending the group in terms of social contact and peer support as well as the impact of the group on those who have left; perhaps they felt they were getting no benefit, or they may have felt that the group had helped them to a stage where they no longer needed to come along.

So, the social impact approach is often understood to be one that focuses on impact, individual, community or social, rather than on quality or process. In Ryan's case, however, this approach would yield not very interesting results. As well as the impact, he needs to know why the group works differently for different people. This brings us to the heart of the social impact approach. On the one hand, you have the project or bit of work you are involved with, and on the other hand, you have the impacts of that project. What connects the two? How do we know that this project leads to this impact?

Some kind of theory of change is necessary to make this connection. A theory of change makes explicit the understandings and assumptions that allow us to make this connection. A logic model is essentially a planning tool that is often used in this regard as a way of spelling out in some detail the links between inputs, outputs, outcomes and impacts. However, there is not always a need to make things so complicated. It is just important to reflect on why and how you think activity and change are linked. So, in Ryan's case, he may be working with a more or less explicit theory of change that says something like: 'Attending social and peer support groups improves the mental wellbeing of those who have been recently bereaved'.

When he reflects on his discussion with the group about the impact of coming to the group, especially those who do not stay for the full length of the group, this theory of change may become more refined: 'Attending social and peer support groups improves the mental wellbeing of those who have been recently bereaved, particularly those who are socially isolated'. Practice and theory have come together to provide a new theoretical understanding that can then inform and improve practice. In Ryan's case, understanding the theory of change and reflecting on how it can best link activity and impacts has allowed him to understand better how and why the group works, and learn how it can be improved and better focused in the future.

In this sense, we are all researchers when we evidence our work in and with communities, creating new theoretical understandings and insights. The importance of sharing these understandings towards collaborative learning are covered in Chapter 10.

Some examples of social outcome approaches

Having explored the value of using social impact studies and unpacked a little some of the basic structure of the approach, we now look at some of the approaches and tools you might want to use. These approaches all share some basic characteristics. As social impacts can in themselves be hard to measure, you often need to come up with indicators that do allow you to measure this change. So, you identify the change or impact you want to measure, you decide on some indicators that will allow you to measure this impact, and you go ahead and explore the extent to which you have reached these indicators.

Outcome wheels

An outcome wheel is a great way of capturing change for an individual or a group. Imagine a wheel with a hub from which a number of spokes radiate outwards. Now write the outcome you want to explore at the centre of the wheel. For Ryan, this might be: 'Improved social contact for recently bereaved people'. On the various spokes of the wheel, place indicators of change. These may be placed in advance or, even better, be discussed and agreed with the individual or group; such participatory approaches can use evidence building as part of the capacity-building process. For Ryan's group, the wheel and indicators might look something like Figure 11.1.

Then the group or individual marks on the spokes the extent to which they have reached this indicator – the nearer the outside of the wheel the closer they have got. This process can then be repeated at some future point to demonstrate distance travelled.

Outcome wheels are quick and easy to use, particularly with individuals and small groups.

Impact mapping

Impact mapping is really a simple form of logic modelling, making clear the links between the different parts and stages of a project or activity. You can work through this process with a group, event or whole community, making clear what the different headings mean and capturing the feedback on a flipchart. The result should be a story of the change that the project has brought about. It can also be highly participatory. Table 11.1 provides a simple example of impact mapping.

Impact mapping can be used at the planning stage of a project as well as the evidence-gathering stage. It is ideal to use with a group or a community on a relatively simple project where not too much detail is needed, as it can be done in one session.

Figure 11.1: Outcome wheel

Table 11.1: Impact mapping

Beneficiaries	Input	Output	Outcome	How you know
The people who may benefit from the project	The resources needed to make the project happen	Beneficiaries taking part in activities	The difference this makes	Indicators of change

Social return on investment and social accounting

Social return on investment (SROI) and social accounting have much in common in the way they show social impact. They share common principles and similar stages in their approach. Both aim for a rigour and comprehensiveness that is missing from other approaches. Because of these aims, they both require resources in terms of time and skills that other approaches do not necessarily involve.

Both approaches follow a broadly similar structure:

- planning stage in which the organisation is explored – its stakeholders, its beneficiaries, the changes it aims to bring about and how it does this. An impact map can be the result of this stage;
- evidence-gathering and analysis stage in which evidence is collected to report on impact;
- reporting and verification stage in which a report is drawn up and verified.

SROI

SROI most distinctively attaches a financial value to the understanding and measuring of change. This attaching of financial value allows for the capturing of impact from a range of stakeholders while at the same time calculating an overall value.

This translating of value into financial terms allows for the calculation of a ratio of benefits to costs. For example, if £5 of social value is created for every £1 invested, we have a ratio, or a social return on investment, of 5:1. Of course, some changes are hard to value in monetary terms. However, it is important to value them, or they may get lost when an assessment of overall impact is made. This valuing of all stakeholders' perspectives is important, as it gives a particular emphasis to the value from the perspective of participants or beneficiaries, a perspective that may, unfortunately, often be ignored in this process.

SROI is also much more than these financial valuations or the final ratio; it is the testing of the theory of change, an analysis of how change occurs for a given organisation and its work that is just as significant. The following case study shows how the financial valuations support the theory of change:

Tom works for a local council in a rural area, managing a capacity-building project working with older people. In a context of increasing numbers of older people alongside pressures on health and social care services, the aim of the project is to support communities and older people in particular to create and run their own activities and services for older people. The project commissions an evaluation using an SROI approach. The study establishes as the project's key theory of change that engagement in the physical and social activities set up by the project will mean older people are less likely to require health and social care supports in future. Although the study cannot test this theory definitively (because of the long-term nature of the changes), its rigorous collection of feedback in relation to outcomes from a range of stakeholders resulted in an SROI ratio of 5:1. It strongly suggests, therefore, that investment in such long-term development work does have an impact on the use of other services. Funders were impressed by this ratio – they were looking for a ratio of 3:1 for any projects to receive further funding. Tom and other stakeholders in the project gained valuable understanding of what was working and why, and that the theory of change could only be properly tested over a longer period of time.

Attaching a financial value to the changes discussed is what is most distinctive and also most controversial about SROI. There is a range of methods, taken from economic evaluation and, more recently, from work on subjective wellbeing valuation, that can inform this financial valuation. For some changes, the financial valuation seems relatively straightforward. For example, if someone is not using a particular service because of an intervention, this would seem to result in a cost saving to these services. Some other changes are not so obviously able to be valued. How can one value a personal change such as improved social contact, for example? Bearing in mind distinctions between the kinds of things to be valued, financial proxies have been attached to each outcome or change. The proxies should be discussed as far as possible with each stakeholder and are based, again as far as possible, on previous SROIs or other research.

As well as the financial proxies, there are other considerations to take into account in measuring the social impact. Deadweight describes what would have happened regardless of the work of the intervention. Attribution is about the contribution of factors other than the work of the project to the changes. Duration describes the extent of the impact over time after the intervention. Finally, there is displacement, the negative changes that may occur as a result of the activity. These can all be calculated to some extent using previous research, but assumptions will also clearly have to be made. These assumptions need to be made explicit.

Let us see how this might work in practice, from the perspective of a project's beneficiaries.

Fifteen people coming to Ryan's group report improved social contact. Using membership of a social club worth £50 as a financial proxy, or substitute, for this improved social contact, we can say that the total financial value of this improvement is 15 x 50 = 750. Here we need to bring in deadweight/attribution/displacement. Deadweight is calculated at 10% based on the surveys that show most users do not go out and meet people anyway; attribution is also calculated at 10% because the survey shows that most users do not have significant, regular input from other people. Duration is probably not a factor here. It would be limited to the lifetime of the group unless it could be shown that friendships are formed that will carry on after the group. There is no apparent displacement; 20% of 750 is 150 so the end value here is 600. Outcomes from the perspective of other stakeholders, such as health and social care services and families, will also be considered and given a financial valuation before coming up with an overall ratio.

The SROI analysis is then produced in a report that is inspected and verified by a panel.

For some stakeholders, funders in particular, this headline ratio figure may be of particular interest. It may also be used, as suggested earlier, by the organisation for promotional purposes. For Ryan, however, what is probably most useful about this process will be the testing of his theory of change connecting the inputs, outputs and outcomes. The analysis shows that for a certain investment in particular activity, a particular outcome will occur that can be a given a value. This is a powerful argument.

Social accounting

Social accounting is a longer-established process than SROI. It is based on the understanding that social value should be reported on and audited just as we report on financial performance. It shares the same basic stages as SROI as outlined in the previous section but does not necessarily involve giving a financial value to social value. Qualitative evidence of social value can stand as it is without also being given a financial value. An SROI analysis can, however, be part of the social accounts.

Key to social accounting is that it is regular so that the concept and the practice becomes embedded in the culture of the organisation. This regularity provides a means whereby the organisation can compare its own performance year on year and against appropriate external norms or benchmarks, and provides for comparisons to be made between organisations doing similar work and reporting in similar fashion. Finally, the accounts need to be verified just as financial accounts are verified by a suitably qualified panel.

When to use SROI or social accounting approaches

The scope of an SROI report or a set of social accounts can vary greatly, from covering a particular project to encompassing the work of a whole organisation. Regardless of their scope, however, both approaches take some time in terms of planning and execution. They need commitment from all parts of the organisation and particular skills in those leading on the process. As more comprehensive approaches than outcome wheels or impact mapping, they are capable of capturing change in a more multifaceted way.

Choosing the right tool

There are some practical issues associated with using social impact studies. As the earlier examples show, there are a range of tools at your disposal. It is important to choose the right tool for the project or activity in question, or the process could be quite resource-intensive. What is appropriate for the activity will depend on the activity itself, your own skills and resources and, equally important, what you want to achieve with the impact study, as the following case study shows.

> Martha wants a quick way to evidence the impact on people with mental health problems of attending a women's group that she supports. She decides to capture information from everyone who comes individually rather than as a group as some members are unlikely to speak up in the group. She uses outcome wheels and encourages everyone to come up with their own indicators. She does this round about the time people start the group and also after six months, to capture the distance travelled by the individual.

Measurement

A further consideration in choosing the most effective approach is that whichever tool you use has a bearing on the actual measurement of impact. Measurement, as explained in the introduction to this chapter, is a tricky thing. It is really only useful if it can appeal to some common framework that allows for comparisons. With so many different tools and approaches, this common framework becomes difficult. In addition, even those who are using the same tool may struggle to make meaningful comparisons. For example, SROI's use of financial proxies as a measurement of social impact allows it to make to produce an SROI ratio that often becomes the headline of the study – for every x number of pounds invested in the project you get 3x back in terms of social value. However, no one would be confident of using this investment ratio on its own as the basis for comparison between projects. There are just too many variables within projects, and within the process of the study itself, that make this comparison fairly meaningless. This is not to say that the investment ratio is worthless; merely that it needs to be understood within the broader story of change evidenced by any good demonstration of impact. It is sometimes said that not everything that is of value can be measured. We are not sure this is true. Rather, it is that measurement can only take us so far in understanding social value in any context. We must be realistic about the extent of measurement in social impact approaches and embed them in the particularities and richness of their own contexts.

Theory of change

As discussed earlier, there is some kind of theory of change that underpins social impact approaches, even if this is not widely articulated. This theory of change may be controversial, or at least provisional, and should be made explicit.

Let us return again to Ryan and the bereavement group. After talking to group members, he has already revised his theory of change to: 'Attending social and peer support groups improves the mental wellbeing of those who have been recently bereaved, particularly those who are socially isolated'. But this theory of change should itself be up for revision in the light of new evidence, gathered both from the group and other, broader, related research. This revision and improvement of the theory of change can only happen if it is explicit and understood as a theory of change.

Attribution

Often in community work, the factors affecting change are various and hard to disentangle. It is usually hard to claim clear attribution for a set of impacts from one particular activity. SROI has ways of estimating the attribution that may sometimes be useful, but could equally be misleading. The fact that attribution is in many situations hard to articulate precisely should not stop organisations and practitioners looking to show evidence of their impact. It is an encouragement to work better with other organisations, not just on the planning and delivery of projects, but also on the gathering of evidence of their impact.

Participatory approaches

Chapter 2 of this book stresses the importance of voice, of having both the opportunity and capacity to frame and articulate one's own experience. Participatory approaches are a way of allowing for voice in evidencing impact. For example, in the earlier discussion of outcome wheels, it is the participants who choose the outcome indicators; in this way, the evidence of impact is led by their own lived experience. This participatory approach means not only that the evidence gathered is likely to be better evidence and not distorted by a professional's preconceptions and assumptions, but also that the gathering of evidence becomes part of the capacity-building process. It adds to the value of it, rather than being external, which makes sense to participants, practitioners and managers.

This allowing for voice in evidencing impact is very important and is underpinned by an awareness of how one's own positionality can hinder the voice of others. You will always have some position in the world and some set of views that defines this position. Critical reflection is crucial in ensuring that these views do not limit the opportunities for other to express their own views.

Challenge questions

1. What is the value of the impact of your work you wish to capture? Can all values be measured?
2. Who, what and why do you want to influence with the impact study?
3. What is the theory of change underpinning the work you wish to evidence?
4. What is the capacity of your organisation to measure social impact and what resources are available?

References

Arvidson, M. and Lyon, F. (2014) Social impact measurement and non-profit organisations: compliance, resistance, and promotion, *VOLUNTAS: International Journal of Voluntary and Nonprofit Organizations*, 25(4): 869–86.

Maas, K.E.H. (2009) *Social Impact Measurement: A Classification of Methods*, Working Paper, Rotterdam: Erasmus University Rotterdam.

Marx, K. (1990) *Das Kapital* (trans. B. Fowkes), London: Penguin.

12

The long haul: longitudinal studies

Karen McArdle and Catherine McKay

Introduction

Often with work in the community, we know that the impact of the work will be long term rather than short term. Often, however, funding and political concerns require that we show evidence of impact at the end of a short-term funding period. It is often the case that we meet people who say that if it hadn't been for our intervention, their life would have been a disaster. This is evidence of impact in the long term. If, as is the case for many of the social professions, such as youth work, community work, social work or adult education, we work knowing that people may not fully realise the change that has occurred until later on in their lives, we need to consider longitudinal studies. For those who operate exclusively in the short term, the types of initiative that have a long-term impact are those which work with vulnerable groups of people or that seek attitude and behavioural change, such as growth in self-esteem and agency. We can, of course, gather evidence in the short term, but sometimes the high quality and richness of development over time is worth seeking out.

This chapter seeks to explain longitudinal studies to equip you with an understanding of how to implement them yourself as well as commission them from other people, as they can be time and resource-intensive. They are important to the credibility of what we do in the human professions and we aim to show you ways in which they can be used to gather evidence in retrospect as well as during your project.

Sometimes short-term evidence is a snapshot in time and sometimes positive evidence is dismissed as the feel-good factor after an activity or intervention. Accordingly, longitudinal evidence is seen as more robust; the value placed on it is higher and so it is viewed, rightly or wrongly, as being more plausible. It therefore has more power to convince funders, decision makers and policy makers. Often done by academics, longitudinal studies are well regarded, but this book is aimed at practitioners, so we intend to show how this work can be done by those working outside the university or college setting. In this regard, we emphasise retrospective studies, which are studies that look back over time to assess impact. We return to these later in the chapter.

Theory

In thinking about longitudinal studies, it is important to be clear about what we mean by long. One well-known longitudinal study is Growing Up in Scotland, which is a cohort study tracking the lives of thousands of children and their families from the early years, through childhood and beyond. The main aim of the study is to provide new information to support policy making in Scotland, but it is also intended to provide a resource for practitioners, academics, the voluntary sector and parents. We may think of longitudinal studies as lasting five years or more, but this again is a questionable measure, in that five years is short in a lifespan but long for an intervention in some areas of the human services. If we conduct a longitudinal study over a shorter period of time than this, the intervention assessed is likely to be intense and sustained. There is no consensus or authoritative agreement on exactly how long a study should last to be considered longitudinal, and at least a year is usual but by no means necessary.

Longitudinal studies characteristically explore major changes in feelings or perceptions – what we term change in behaviour and being. Longitudinal studies are often quantitative for a range of reasons, not least because they seek to measure change over time. They are by no means always quantitative and, for the worker in the community, a qualitative study is often more accessible and relevant as it concerns people and behaviour in a complex environment. For this reason, we focus here largely on qualitative approaches, although most longitudinal studies for gathering evidence use a mix of quantitative and qualitative elements, as well as open and closed questions.

Exactly what constitutes change is also an interesting question that underpins this book. We consider that change is from a trajectory to 'something different', and that 'something different' is hopefully something positive. The change, in the context of this book, occurs for a reason other than normal human development; we seek change that is a product of an intervention, series of interventions, or a complex of intervention and normal human growth, whatever we take that to be. The person who decides whether that change has occurred is often the learner, client or member of the public with whom we have been working. We suggest that this should usually be the case, although a case may be made for the opinion of the family or associates, as well as the expert view of the worker in the community. The latter opinion would not be very strong, we suggest, without the opinion of the others. Change is often the product of a range of factors and may be disjointed and multifaceted, as well as featuring interrelated variables. This means it can be very difficult to measure, which is one of the reasons why we need to seek the perspective of the person or people at the centre of what we do or have done. There is no doubt that change can be cataclysmic, or sudden on occasion, but in many fields, change takes time and patience for the full implications to be realised.

If you decide to commission or indeed conduct a longitudinal study, you must be clear about both time and change. You should decide on the time course and the change you seek to explore. As will become clear, we hope, in longitudinal studies there is plenty of potential for change that is unpredicted and unexpected, so it is important to be prepared for this. We would argue that it is impossible to use numbers to measure change in a way that evidences the effectiveness of a human programme. You can count the number of people who attend a programme or the number of people who attain qualifications or continue to other destinations, but because such factors are interrelated, emergent and complex you can only measure them superficially. If you wish to seek evidence of effectiveness, we recommend that you use either qualitative or mixed methods. Mixed methods blend and triangulate quantitative and qualitative methods.

Commissioning a longitudinal study is expensive, especially if it involves universities or colleges. Developing links with such institutions is often a means for generating long-term studies and external expertise, as many academic researchers value the context in which to do research as a quid pro quo for doing a study that is of value to the practitioner. Practitioners may, of course, also be researchers; it is not as difficult as it sounds. One way of doing this is with training and support from universities, as in a practitioner-led action research model. This is where universities are funded to introduce groups of practitioners to research methods, and support them to identify which area of work to focus on and write up their work and research findings. The following case study demonstrates the role of research in validating the findings of a long-term family learning project.

> Robert was instrumental in setting up a family learning project in an area of multiple deprivation. The aim was to work with primary schools to identify and encourage fathers and their children to be involved in group activities with other fathers and children. Over 150 fathers and 300 children participated over the eight years of the project.
>
> Over the years, the project team noticed significant increases in confidence and self-efficacy for some men. Fathers who were quiet and on the fringes of the project when they first got involved gradually became more active by, for example, serving on the organising committee of the project or taking up opportunities to improve their own skills. The team's observations were anecdotal and not validated externally in any way until Robert decided to undertake a master's degree qualification and use his work with the project as the subject for his dissertation.

His research used qualitative methodology with face-to-face interviews with a small number of fathers triangulated by focus groups. The research benefitted from the fact that Robert had established rapport and trust with the fathers who were willing to participate.

Much family learning research shows benefits for children. This research was able, however, to show the benefits for fathers in terms of confidence, self-efficacy and social capital over time.

Methods

Methods of undertaking longitudinal studies are very diverse but some methods lend themselves to long-term projects in particular. One of the key principles of longitudinal studies is that they have a 'then and now' dimension. If one is to identify change over time, one needs to know the status of a situation at the 'then' moment. Put more simply, the enquirer needs a benchmark for how things were before or at the start of an intervention. This can then be linked to how things are now and the difference analysed.

Such a benchmark can be discovered in many ways, for example through observation, interviews, questionnaires and other well-known methods. The principal difference with longitudinal studies is that they are analysed differently from other studies, with the emphasis on change over time as illustrated by difference, patterns and trends. The questions that lead to this analysis may be framed slightly differently from questions in more short-term research. These questions, outlined by Saldana (2003: 67), may be summarised as follows:

1. What is different from one cycle of findings to the next?
2. When have changes occurred through time?
3. What factors have influenced or affected people over time?
4. How has the participant changed over time?
5. What preliminary analysis can be made as the study progresses?

Data analysis grows over time and the questions to ask of the data are no different from those of any other study, where we look for similarities, differences, patterns, trends, halts and absences. The difference in longitudinal studies is that we look over time. A second subtle difference is that new, unexpected, things may emerge over time, and we must account for these.

Saldana (2003: 103) discusses development, pointing to one of its difficulties and, we would add, some of its beautiful aspects:

> The word 'development' implies more qualitative characteristics across time, such as improvement, betterment, and transformation. Developmental variables are more ephemeral, socially constructed, not accessible to precise measurement, and include such concepts as knowledge, empathy, worldview, aesthetic response, and values.

Longitudinal studies also characteristically have cycles of inquiry, whereby intermittent points of analysis are implemented, so that patterns and trends on a trajectory are determined prior to a final analysis. Cumulative effects of data must be taken into account in longitudinal studies and triangulation of data over time enhances its strength and robustness.

There are dimensions of analysis that are particular to analysis of longitudinal studies. Derived again from Saldana (2003: 127), we pose four specific questions that show the difference of these studies from the usual snapshot pictures we may take in our studies.

1. Which changes interrelate through time?
2. Which changes through time are part of or different from natural human development?
3. Which changes are part of or different from constructed social processes?
4. What are participants' phases, stages or cycles?

The second question is arguably the most important of these, as well as being the most difficult to decide. Exactly what constitutes natural human development is hard to decide for anyone. We need simply to distinguish between what is a product of our activity and what would have happened anyway.

'Early', 'middle' and 'later' are concepts we might use to trace a trajectory in longitudinal research and to trace changes over time. An example is given in Box 11.1.

Box 11.1 Tracing a trajectory

Before – she was depressed about being unemployed and because of issues with literacy saw no way out of this situation.

Middle – she met a friend who had similar difficulties and they enrolled together in a group that sought to assist people with literacy issues.

Later – she grew in confidence and saw the possibilities of improving her skills with the ultimate goal of seeking employment. She felt much happier in herself.

Retrospective studies

A retrospective study returns to the individual or group comprising the target of an intervention or activity, and seeks to gather evidence of the long-term impact of the historical activity on people's lives. This is an excellent means of finding out, on reflection and over time, what has happened to people's lives from what they have experienced or learnt.

As the term longitudinal refers to time and the change over time, we have chosen to discuss retrospective studies here. A retrospective study looks back at a period of time, again probably a long period of time, for evidence-gathering purposes. It considers change over time in exactly the same way as a longitudinal study except that it generates evidence in retrospect. We have all met an individual a long time after completing an activity or intervention who says, "If it hadn't been for you …". A retrospective study simply captures this evidence in a way that looks to the beginning, middle and later part of an intervention, but is conducted after the intervention has ended.

Accordingly, it is possible to find people who have long left an intervention and to ask them to say how it affected their life, if at all, and how they feel about it now. Finding one person allows you to find others by asking them if they are still in contact with anyone else from the activity. As practitioners, we often use this method to evaluate long-term activities and find that narrative inquiry is the best method to use, being accessible and akin to natural storytelling. Narrative inquiry, discussed further in Chapter 9, is a means of asking a limited number of questions that invite the participant to tell the story of their life. The inquirer might begin by asking, "Can you tell me about the first time you heard about the project?", and follow this up with questions such as, "What did you think at first?" and "How did you feel?". The questions progress to discussing later life and whether it still had an impact. There is a skill in inviting people to reflect on their lives and it requires you to be non-judgemental and engaging, perhaps sharing aspects of your life to emulate the giving required by the participant.

There are inevitably criticisms of this means of gathering evidence, as there are of all such measures, but it is an authentic and thoughtful means of finding out about long-term change. The criticisms centre on how well people remember the intervention and how accurately they tell the story of their lives. People inevitably frame their life stories in ways that show them in a particular light, not necessarily always positive. Short of discussing what reality actually is, whether it exists independently of us or whether it only exists in the individual's way of seeing it, we have found that it acceptable in such situations to take what is told to us to be the truth as the participant perceives it.

As with any other kind of study, sample size can be variable, but is better if there are a number of people involved, albeit each person's experience is unique and does not lend itself to comparison except insofar as it reflects on the activity or intervention. Narrative inquiry typically uses a small number of respondents, commonly between one and five people, for example. For gathering evidence of effectiveness, a larger number is desirable, although the outcome for Jim in participating in the Scottish educational programme Reach Out, described in Chapter 9, was a worthwhile outcome of itself.

Clearly a retrospective case study can be used once a project has been established without the luxury of a pre-established benchmark, but both Jim, as described in Chapter 9, and Alasdair in the following example, provide their own idiosyncratic benchmarks. For Jim, it was "dog eat dog"; for Alasdair, it was being a street drinker.

> Alasdair (not his real name) is an intelligent Scottish man of around 30 years of age who has substance misuse issues – mainly, but not exclusively, alcohol. He has been a street drinker and has a history of begging. He started participating in the project five years earlier and continues to do so. The project seeks to help people take the first steps that lead to employment or other worthwhile lifestyles. He looked back over his time with the project:
>
> '[The project] helps improve what are often bleak lives.'
>
> Alasdair described how he was socially isolated prior to coming to the project, but his attendance helped him set on a different path. It provided structure in his life and gave him a reason to get up in the morning and not have a drink:
>
> 'Even when I was down and out, even when I was drinking heavily, I always cam [came] here sober. Being here meeting people it helps build confidence. Brought me right oot meself [out of myself]. Makes me confident with people. Makes me look at things from another perspective.'

One of the interesting things about this case study is the mix of speech tenses that the participant, Alasdair, uses to signal beginning, middle and later.

Strengths and limitations

The strengths of longitudinal studies lie in their robustness through the triangulation of data over time, which provides substantial and convincing data that appeal to funders and policy makers. The limitations of such studies is that they require both cost and staff commitment and can be time-consuming. Both a potential strength and limitation is the extent to which such studies require engagement with the participants or clients. If people are going to commit to a long process, you must engage with them well. The depth and robustness of this kind of evidence gathering is linked to the quality of community engagement required.

Similarly, both a strength and limitation lie in the need for your participants, population or clients to be self-reflective in order to engage with the changes that have occurred in their lives over time and may not always be positive. You should always be clear at the start of a longitudinal study exactly what is required of the participant and how this will be achieved. Self-reflection demands that you as inquirer must be sensitive to the consequences of this reflection on a life lived, not always lived as the individual concerned may have preferred. Ethically, a participant should always have the right to withdraw. To assist participants to be self-reflective, we suggest, you should be reflective yourself to enable them to consider their life in a careful, critical and truthful manner.

Ethics is particularly important for longitudinal or retrospective studies, as is data protection legislation in many countries. To ask people to participate longitudinally is to make a significant demand on their time, and we should be cognisant of this fact. Countries with data protection legislation often demand that demographic information and data relating to people's opinion are not kept beyond a certain point in time or for certain purposes. You should be aware of such requirements in your country, as they prevent you from requesting certain information, such as notice of change of address. Longitudinal studies also make emotional demands on people's time and energy. Without strong motivation on their part or strong engagement on your part, people will not participate. People often enjoy talking about their life, but the complexity of daily life can often get in the way.

Importantly, ethics demands that participants have the right to withdraw at any stage of a research project. At a practical level, if you are planning a study you should allow in your sample for a certain level of participant drop-out that will inevitably occur. Incentives for participation are another important consideration. Payment for participation is controversial, but at the very least there should be refreshments and respect for participants' contribution.

We have referred to engagement as being important for securing participation, but it is difficult to explain what we mean by this. An ability to engage demands personal qualities that seek to value participants, to listen in a non-judgemental way to what they have to say, and to acknowledge all contributions positively. Moreover, it involves inquirers giving something of themselves in order to encourage open communication.

We conclude by encouraging you to engage with longitudinal work, as we consider it to be largely missing from some very effective long-term and intensive interventions. We know such interventions are effective over time, but find it hard to evidence this fact other than with assertion. Politicians, policy makers and funders need to know that big differences can be made to people's lives through work in the community.

Challenge questions

1. Who would you need to persuade if you wanted to carry out a longitudinal study of the impact of your work?
2. What are the ethical considerations you should think about before embarking on a longitudinal study?
3. How would you secure professional learning opportunities for practitioners who wish to practise action learning research/ conduct a retrospective study?

Reference
Saldana, J. (2003) *Longitudinal Qualitative Research: Analyzing Change Through Time*, Walnut Creek, CA: Altamira Press.

13

What everyone needs to know: management information systems

Sue Briggs, Kirsty Forrester and Karen McArdle

Introduction

> A female community worker, Marion, is interested in who participates in her town's community centres. She consults the organisation's management information system (MIS) and discovers that her perceptions and suspicions of gender bias are accurate. The participants are 78% female and over the age of 65. She decides to run some dads' groups that target younger men with school-age children.

In this example, a community worker has used an MIS for needs analysis to confirm what was originally just suspicion. An MIS may be characterised as a repository for key information that helps an organisation keep itself on track. It is a secure and safe way used by organisations to record the personal information of clients, participants or service users. The word management is often considered to be a noun in the MIS phrase; it implies that the system is for a particular group of people – managers. We suggest it should be a verb and is a system about the process of management for all people in an organisation.

The information a system retains is most often quantitative and most often electronic, though not necessarily so. Paper systems do exist and often MISs act as a repository for some qualitative information, such as qualitative evaluation findings or records of progress/achievement. It is referred to as a system because it implies a wide coverage of information and a comprehensive approach to gathering information. In short, it does not work if there are holes in it, a topic we return to later in this chapter. MISs do not need to be large and complex. Many people have paper systems or use Excel or other forms of spreadsheet. The advantage of having an electronic system is that it can be accessed by other people. If you have a paper system in a filing cabinet and go off sick, nobody can access the information if the cabinet is kept locked, as it should be if it contains people's data. Moreover, paper systems are usually only easily accessible to the people who have devised them.

Many local authorities collect huge amounts of administrative data that you can use for evidence, even if this does not constitute an MIS. Such secondary data are discussed in more detail in Chapter 14.

MISs and the community worker: how to use the system

Although this is a 'how to' book, all MISs are different and we cannot begin to illustrate how to use any single, particular system. We simply exhort you to make use of a resource that can underpin every dimension of your work. An MIS has a feedback loop, in that the more you put into it and convince others to do the same, the more you get out of it. The argument, often used in community work, that time is not sufficient to use MISs, suggests to us that priorities need to be re-examined, as the information such systems can potentially provide is one half of the statistics and stories needed to demonstrate the impact of what we do. We need to demonstrate to ourselves, to the organisation and to the community that our work is worthwhile, value for money, effective and has impact; MISs can help us do this more easily. If the system is clunky, this needs to be fed back to management, taking into account that the system may need to work for a range of professionals in community and other work.

Ten key steps underpin the use of MISs for community work, as follows:

- Decide what you would like to know.
- Find out whether the system is set up to collect the data.
- Plan how this information may be collected.
- Consult the relevant manager/technician about whether or how the system could do this.
- Consider practical and ethical implications of collecting the information.
- Convince others of the need/desirability of collecting the information.
- Devise and circulate guidance on what information to collect.
- Conduct training on what needs to be collected.
- Set up and use the system.
- When information is no longer useful, arrange for its collection to stop.

Assuming you are disposed to participate in the use of the MIS, you should adopt the following key procedures:

- Scrutinise guidance on what information is needed and in what form.
- Plan when to gather the information and in what form.
- Devise means of gathering information for your own projects that are appropriate for the purpose and make minimal demands on participants, clients or users (literacy may be an issue if using forms or questionnaires, for example).
- Gather the necessary information and store it reliably and confidentially.
- Enter the data into the system carefully.
- Check carefully what you have entered.
- If the system is electronic, destroy the paper records for ethical reasons.

The collection of information is not an end in itself. The purpose of gathering information is to improve practice in the following ways, although this is not an exhaustive list and you may well be able to think of more:

- Conduct a needs analysis.
- Generate a picture of the demographics of participants.
- Identify patterns/trends/omissions in the engagement of participants.
- Illustrate the experience/transition/progression of participants.
- Monitor progress and drop-out.
- Assess the impact of services/interventions.
- Evaluate the numeric dimensions of services.
- Demonstrate evidence of the scale of work undertaken.
- Conduct performance review and monitoring.
- Monitor staff ratios, workload and value for money of services.
- Prepare for supervision/mentoring sessions.
- Plan new services.
- Pilot new services.
- Support funding applications.
- Prepare annual reports.
- Support presentations concerning services.

Ethical considerations

Ethical considerations are, of course, very important. From a practical point of view, there is no reason to gather information if you are not going to use it. You should explain the reasons for gathering information and saving it to the person concerned and, where possible, do so with a guarantee of anonymity and/or confidentiality. In a more philosophical vein, you should also consider the rights of the person whose information you are collecting and storing. Here the concept of beneficence is important – that we are doing this with the public 'good' in mind – but who is defining the public 'good' and what exactly does this mean? Beneficence, we would argue, covers the purposes of needs analysis, monitoring, reviewing and, above all, assessing the impact of what we do in community work, which itself aims to improve wellbeing for individuals and groups.

Interpretation of the information derived from MISs is very complex and has an ethical dimension. We should be truthful in how we present the data; we should not give it a positive spin if it is negative, for example, as this would not be not truthful. We should be both balanced and objective to some extent (we say to some extent, as we would argue that objectivity and subjectivity are on a continuum and are not absolutes). Sometimes we are surprised by MISs and we need to take the bad with the good. Exactly how we present findings can be very complex, as we work in complex domains. What if the information shows negative racial characteristics, for example? What if the political leader's flagship project fails to meet its stated objectives? Ethical problems do not have right or wrong answers; we must, however, think carefully about anything that troubles us and if we find ourselves manipulating findings, we should be alert to the fact that there is an ethical problem.

We should also ask who owns the information given to us by members of the public. Many countries have legislation that determines what can be stored and the degree of confidentiality that must be maintained. Aside from this, McNiff and colleagues (2018: 804) talk about the contingency of practice, a view we share: 'Practices should be seen as contingent, situated in a wider cultural, historical, social and political discourses, and should be interrogated in relation to whose interests they potentially serve'.

This illustrates the perspective that MISs need to be used in a way that is consistent with the principles that underpin work in the community. McNiff and colleagues (2018) go on to criticise the idea that 'official knowers' are qualified to think and act in relation to practice. We suggest that MISs run the risk of making some people 'official knowers' and that care should be taken to think about who owns the information, who has access to it and what for, and what is the role of the community in understanding the information they have given. Once again, we find McNiff and colleagues (2018: 804) useful in underpinning this community practice issue:

> We argue throughout that all participants' local knowledge is core to any understanding of practice, whether in health care, teacher education or international development. We further argue that the aim of all development work should be to promote independent thought and action with a view to achieving personal and social independence….

This quotation illustrates the ultimate aim of practice and we would argue that the dimensions come together to form practice, of which MISs are a part. We should be cognisant of the ultimate goals of what we do the implications of all that we do to meet these goals. Similarly, as discussed in the introduction, the meaning of concepts such as impact and quality cannot be seen as neutral or decontextualised in the way that numbers and statistics are often viewed. Numbers are valued highly in our society but although they may illustrate impact, they do so in a way that is always contingent on individuals' and collectives' interests, and these interests usually are socially constructed and stray into orthodoxy (McArdle, 2018; McNiff et al, 2018).

What this means for community workers is that they should report MIS findings in a way that is honest and truthful and conscious of both context and the ultimate aims of their practice. In turn, we argue, this means that local people should be involved in both setting criteria for quality and impact on their lives and in finding out the information that has been processed about them. This does not, of course, mean finding out confidential information about others, but they have a right to know the outcome of the findings to which they have contributed.

Legal considerations

To protect people's rights and privacy, many countries have legislation that determines what data can and cannot be held. Here we provide a summary of the principles that underpin the legislation in the UK and apply to us in our work as community practitioners.

There are eight principles of good information handling outlined in the UK's Data Protection Act 2018. These state that data must be:

• fairly and lawfully processed;
• processed for limited purposes;
• adequate, relevant and not excessive;
• accurate;
• not kept for longer than is necessary;
• processed in line with an individual's rights;

- secure;
- not transferred to other countries without adequate protection.

Personal data are becoming increasingly valuable, and the collectors and users of data have responsibilities under the Act, such as asking a data subject's permission to use their data. It is important that you familiarise yourself with your country's data protection legislation, if this exists, as well as any relevant international legislation.

Pros and cons of MISs

There are arguably three categories of organisational benefit to using MISs – strategic, informational and transactional (Mirani and Lederer, 1998). In terms of the public sector and third sector, strategy assists with decision making and planning. Informational benefits apply at all levels of the organisation, ensuring that professionals make better-informed judgements about practice. Finally, transaction benefits are that the services provided to communities and individuals within those communities are better informed. MISs, we argue, also contribute to improved financial judgements and decision making; a better experience for the participant, client or community in terms of service quality; improved internal performance on the part of the organisation; and, importantly, the learning, innovation, growth and development of the organisation in a complex service environment.

MISs are underpinned by certain assumptions, not least that counting things matters. It also assumes that there are things that can be counted, and that this process is valuable. Counting things does matter, we suggest. In a youth agency, for example, one could make comparative judgements about a service that involves five young people and two staff and a drop-in service for 30 young people and one staff member. The context and performance against established priorities will determine the judgements we make, but we need primary data to make them. Some things in community work cannot be counted, we suggest, such as trust and growth in self-esteem, but the numbers of people engaging in programmes linked to these qualities can be counted. Similarly, the progression from one service to another can be tracked. A third assumption is linked to the character of professionals and what they wish to monitor, track, analyse and improve. We suggest that this assumption has to be valid and that all workers in the community should and must make use of the opportunities that MISs offer. MISs contain primary data from a wide range of sources and have the potential to contribute positively to the work of individuals within an organisation. They provide an opportunity to look beyond the day-to-day work in the community to see the bigger picture, which is both informative in many dimensions, and, we suggest, exciting. They can provide data for funding, evaluation, demonstrating impact, and, we would add, credibility, which is often linked, whether we agree with it or not, to numerical proof of effectiveness in times of austerity.

The following case study shows how one of us, Kirsty Forrester, used an MIS known as SEEMIS to inform practice with parents:

> I requested a report from SEEMIS (an MIS for schools) about the number of children in Dundee's schools requiring English as additional language support. This highlighted the number of children who had English as an additional language, but we could also deduce from it that their parents probably had ESOL (English for Speakers of Other Languages) needs, so we used this information to look at areas and schools that would potentially benefit from support services. We then commissioned Dundee's International Women's Centre to deliver family learning in some of the schools with the highest needs, in partnership with school and family support workers. We share this information with our partners, who use the information to highlight the needs of the community in Dundee when applying for funding.

Kirsty used the MIS at a number of levels – to determine a demographic; to establish need; to extrapolate data for the identification of associated needs; and to support future funding applications. MISs vary in quality and, clearly, it is important for an organisation to have the best system it can afford. Planning what the system is wanted for and, accordingly, what is to be entered into it, is, of course, critical to maintaining its accuracy and quality. Once this has been decided, usually by managers, guidelines should be drafted to indicate exactly what is to be included so that the relevant information is included by all people involved in data entry. So, for example, if you count participants who engage with a community event, it could be a thousand people, or if you count the number who actually sign up to a service at the same event it could be, say, 30. All people who enter information must count the same thing. Systems are not always user-friendly. This is partly because they often collect information from a range of professions who may use different terms to describe similar things. Moreover, systems are not always designed by those who will be end users. It is still, however, important and often very simple to learn how to use them. Users may take some time to become familiar with the language, but data entry is usually linked to quite simple ideas such name, age, date of birth, address, postcode and attendance at a particular service. However, MISs are only useful if they are used to generate reports, so another level of data is required. Again, this usually comprises simple counts and percentages, so you do not need a detailed knowledge of statistics, just familiarity with simple commands to find out what you want to know.

Consistent with the principles of community work, it is preferable for all stakeholders to have a say in the amount, quality and kind of information that is held, and there are many ways that the community can be involved in generating the information that gets entered into the system. Participatory approaches to research and consultation offer a means to involve the community in generating, analysing and interpreting information and avoiding accusations of 'big brothering' people's lives. It is important when thinking of benefits to consider the beneficiaries.

The drawback of MISs is that they are often incompatible with each other. Clearly, the ability to cross-refer information on community health and community education would be advantageous. MISs, however, run the danger of perpetuating a 'silo' culture, especially in the public sector. There is also wide variation in the sophistication and comprehensiveness of systems (Learning Connections, 2006). Central collation of information is crucial to maintaining the integrity of the systems, and reporting back to stakeholders, including the community, is vital to the success of this information gathering.

Who should use MISs?

Participation by everyone involved in a given project is fundamental to the success of MISs. In our experience, however, those working in the community sector, with its emphasis on people skills, sometimes find this difficult. This could be due to an aversion to technology among some people, or because the system is too big and cumbersome. We often hear of community workers who do not have the time to participate in MISs, or of those who find it annoying and boring to do so. We argue that this is a missed opportunity, as MISs have so much potential to influence the quality and credibility of our work, and that it is crucial to participate in good MISs that deliver such benefits. It is not the case that MISs are for managers only. Logic models often underpin MISs, as the following case study shows.

> Jane was asked to facilitate a day session for a charity that supports people with mental health difficulties. She was told by the manager that the staff team and the board had different understandings of the charity's purpose and that these differences were creating difficulties in planning for the future, especially with the existing funding cycle coming to an end.
>
> Jane used a logic model to structure the day. A logic model can take various forms but is essentially a tool for planning that connects need, inputs, outputs and outcomes. The focus of the day was on agreeing outcomes, the differences that the charity aims to make for its beneficiaries. With these agreed on (and set within the larger strategic policy context),

what the charity did and what it needed to do (its outputs and inputs) fitted neatly into place fairly quickly. Agreement on outcomes meant that the whole organisation (staff and board members) could look at how resources and activities could best contribute towards these outcomes. The completed logic model formed the basis for a new business plan for the organisation.

The following extract from an inspection framework for community learning and development in Scotland (Education Scotland, 2016) illustrates good practice in improving performance through good use of information. We argue that these criteria are germane to the role of all professionals who work in a community context:

- Performance information shows improvement in life chances of participants and the wider community.

- Analysis of need is robust. Performance information demonstrates we are achieving challenging targets set and sustaining continuous improvement.

- High quality information and analysis is used consistently and effectively to inform planning and secure improvement. Evidence gathered demonstrates improved outcomes for individuals, groups and communities.

- We share and use information effectively to set challenging targets and secure improvement. There is a strong shared understanding of progress against outcomes and targets.

- We are successful in engaging priority groups identified through needs analysis. There are sustained or increasing levels of involvement and achievement from targeted groups, individuals and communities. (Education Scotland, 2016: 7)

This quotation shows some of the ways in which MISs can be used in work in the community – for example, to show improvement, for needs analysis, for planning and improvement, and for monitoring progress. They can also be used to show sustained, increased and indeed decreased levels of involvement of target groups. With these processes in mind, we should all analyse, monitor and harness the information from MISs.

Exactly how to convince everyone they should participate in MISs is not clear. The higher the quality of the system, the more likely people are to use it (DeLone and McLean, 2003), and the more likely it will impact on the individual's performance and the performance of the organisation. System quality may be measured in terms of its functionality, reliability, flexibility, data quality, portability, integration and importance within the organisation (DeLone and McLean, 2003). It is crucial that this is communicated to community workers so they can see its significance. Information quality may be measured in terms of accuracy, timeliness, completeness, relevance and consistency. The system must be reliable, and community workers should be aware of this. Service quality of any system can be measured in terms of reliability, as already mentioned, as well as responsiveness (promptness) and empathy, the latter being an interesting feature, as it means the system has users' best interests at heart. The system should above all be perceived as benign, having improvement at its heart.

Managers should note that research shows that self-reported use of MISs does not always tally with computer-recorded usage (DeLone and McLean, 2003). Attitudes to using MISs consequently need to change. 'Intention to use' is an attitude, whereas 'use' is a behaviour, and it is important to understand that change is needed at both levels. Use and user satisfaction are closely related, and, arguably, a positive experience of use will lead to further usage. So, a feedback loop is needed, where use is rewarded, perhaps implicitly, but also explicitly.

The quality of information that is complete, easy to understand, personalised, relevant and secure is rewarding in itself to the professional who wishes to make good judgements. However, this needs to be measured against expectations of what is realistic. Kassim and colleagues (2012) discuss the role of trust in uptake of computer systems. They ask whether benevolence, ability and integrity also be ascribed to uptake of, and, indeed, to the technology itself. Trust in technological terms means being behaviourally dependent on a piece of software to do a task. On the one hand, the system must have a benevolent intention, the capacity or ability to do the task and the integrity to do it well and in accordance with benevolence. This makes the system trustworthy. On the other hand, individual community workers require a benevolence of mind, the ability to use the software and the integrity to use it well.

Increasingly, MISs are being implemented in the public and third sectors. They have long been in existence in the private sector, and have also been used in the public sector in procurement and similar processes for many years, but they are increasingly being introduced to the human services in the public and third sectors. This is because of the 'need to know', so that professionals can be effective in what they do and able to show the impact and effectiveness of what they do. In the public sector, in particular, MISs have a longitudinal importance. Elected members of a government and their policies may have a limited lifespan, often of four years or less, but an MIS allows information to be collected over longer periods of time and so may assist with continuity of assessment of need and outcomes for the community. Similarly, in the third sector, where change in the governance of charitable bodies is a common occurrence, MISs allow organisations to maintain records over a sustained period of time in accordance with fundamental vision and aims.

MISs were invented for the private sector, predominantly to manage sales, customer records and finance. In the public and third sectors and in community work, there are multiple, conflicting and intangible goals. Caudle and colleagues (1991), in an early study of key information systems management issues for the public sector, describe this difference as follows:

> It [public sector] produces 'public good' for problems that should be solved [like crime and poverty], even though these problems may have no known feasible solutions; and it is heavily impacted by politics and bureaucratic red tape. These and other features of

> the public sector make it potentially a much different
> setting for IS [information system] management than
> the private sector. (Caudle et al, 1991: 171)

This difference is crucial because public and third sector technological systems are derived from the private sector, but demand much more complex interpretation than private sector systems. A private sector analysis of sales patterns and trends is arguably much simpler than a pattern and trend of community engagement. The system itself, we argue, is transferable, but the interpretation of context and meaning is much more complex, and we return to this later in the chapter. Much of the literature on MISs concerns how to design them and to implement them at management level. The literature on users and the public and third sectors is sparse. It is a question of practitioners consulting the relevant sources relating to MIS usage in the private sector and translating this information to a new and much more complex environment.

We explore this difference further because it helps illustrate the challenges for MISs in the public and third sectors. Caudle and colleagues (1991) refer to the environmental factors that affect MISs in the US – increased legal and formal constraints, interest groups and constituencies. They also discuss organisational factors – level of scrutiny of public officials, and the expectation that officials act fairly, responsively, accountably and honestly – and, finally, internal structure and processes – managers with less decision-making autonomy, less authority over subordinates and a greater reluctance to delegate.

These factors colour the context of MISs in the public sector 'their multiple and intangible criteria, multiple and conflicting interest groups, and lack of feasible solutions' (Caudle et al, 1991: 175). Top managers in the public sector arguably have a broader external role than their counterparts in private firms. Much of the literature we have read refers to the private sector in terms of customer satisfaction and increasing sales, rather than accountability to the public. We have sought to interpret this for the public and third sectors where most, but not all, community work takes place.

In the third sector, there is probably a need to discuss who owns the data that is kept and the knowledge derived from an MIS. Third sector organisations are often funded by another body with a plausible claim to the data, and there are power implications about who 'owns' this information. MISs in the third sector can be quite small and only relevant to a particular group, so opportunities for sharing data are more limited. As organisations become bigger in the third sector, they may become more professionalised and removed from the communities they support. Small systems, on the other hand, may be close to the community but of limited relevance, so there is a paradox here. Opportunities to share information and data in the third sector are crucial and do exist, but in our experience may be hampered because of the differences and incompatibility between systems. The following case study relates a successful instance of sharing management information that led to a significant piece of new work:

> Martha is a community worker supporting third sector organisations. A series of conversations with various organisations working with vulnerable adults had suggested to her that there was an increasing number of vulnerable adults, often with complex needs, who seemed to be using the services of these organisations, but in an uncoordinated way. Martha organised a meeting of all the organisations, and the information they provided from their individual management information systems confirmed her theory. This evidence was then discussed with public sector partners that also had involvement with vulnerable adults, and there are now regular meetings between all partners to look at how they can work better together to support these vulnerable people.

Our final word concerns the quality of MISs. The system should be accessible and usable, and managers informed if this is not the case. Manager should also be made aware of what changes can be made to enable community workers to make use of the system. In times of austerity, it is vital that community work as a profession shows the importance and relevance of what it does, and MISs can make an important contribution to this purpose.

Challenge questions

1. Is there an MIS at your place of work? If so, how often do you use it? If you do not use it, why not (be honest)? If there is no system, can you think how a simple paper or Excel system could be framed?
2. What reports could you seek from the data in an MIS to assess need?
3. Why do you think many community workers are reluctant to use MISs?

References

Caudle, S.L., Gorr, W.L. and Newcomer, K.E. (1991) Key information systems management issues for the public sector, *MIS Quarterly*, pp 171–188.

DeLone, W. and McLean, E. (2003) The DeLone and McLean model of information systems success: a ten-year update, *Journal of Management Information Systems*, 19(4): 9–30.

Education Scotland (2016) *How Good is the Learning and Development in our Community?: Evaluation Resource*, Livingston: Education Scotland.

Kassim, E.S., Jailani., S.F.A.K., Hairuddin, H. and Zamzuri, N.H. (2012) Information system acceptance and user satisfaction: the mediating role of trust, *Procedia: Social and Behavioural Sciences*, 57: 412–18.

Learning Connections (2008) *Survey of Management Information Systems in Community Learning and Development (CLD)*, Edinburgh: Scottish Government.

McArdle, K. (2018) *Freedom Research in Education: Becoming an Autonomous Researcher*, Cham: Palgrave Macmillan.

McNiff, J., Edvardsen, O. and Steinholt, M. (2018) 'Impact', educational influence and the practice of shared expertise, *Educational Action Research*, 26(5): 803–19.

Mirani, R. and Lederer, A.L. (1998) An instrument for assessing the organizational benefits of IS projects, *Decision Sciences*, 29(4): 803–38.

14

Using others: secondary data

Kirsty Forrester and Karen McArdle

Introduction

Pablo Picasso is a Cubist, one of the founders of a style of painting that abandons perspective with a single viewpoint. On one canvas, for example, he portrayed a chair from many different positions and in many geometric shapes – from above, from below, the legs, the seat. He superimposed these different views to get close to what he thought of as the quintessential truth of a chair. He believed that more than one perspective brought the observer closer to the truth.

We can use a similar approach in community work, specifically with regard to triangulation, which is a key term in this chapter and denotes a way of evidencing our work that combines many different viewpoints. To help explain the concept further, the hill walkers or climbers among you may have heard of trig points, a series of reference points that are used in surveying to determine a fact, such as the height of a mountain. The importance of Picasso and trig points for us is that we can use triangulation in a similar way to obtain more than one point of view about our work in the community. These different points of view help show the validity of any claim we make about our work in the community.

Showing the validity of your claims is crucial, as it may affect your own wellbeing, as well as that of your own work or projects and your participants. Triangulation of evidence gives your work additional credibility over evidence that comes from only one source. In times of austerity, it is particularly important to show that your work is valuable to ensure that it continues; indeed, your own employment may depend on it. The following case study shows how one of us, Kirsty Forrester, triangulated data for employability among Black, Asian and minority ethnic (BAME) people against her own observations.

Box 14.1 Case study for triangulation of evidence

There has been much negative publicity in the UK recently about migrants, including reports that they are a drain on public resources and unemployment benefits. This is certainly not true of the migrants with whom I work regularly. I wanted to get further data on this. I spoke to a data analyst in my organisation to ask if there was any data to confirm high levels of employment among BAME people.

Nomis is a service provided by the Office for National Statistics in the UK that offers free access to detailed and up-to-date UK labour market statistics from official sources. Nomis data showed that there is a higher unemployment rate in the area where I work than in the rest of the country. It also showed that BAME men are more likely to be employed than their white counterparts, while the opposite is true for women. The report showed a low confidence level for nearly all of the data, meaning that the sample size was too small for us to confidently say it was representative of the population. We could, however, compare the information we received against census information, which we know has a very small margin of error even if the data is now out of date. Both datasets told us similar things, which we could triangulate against our own hunches and what the people we work with had told us about their employment status.

(Kirsty Forrester)

Secondary data and secondary literature

We intend in this chapter to distinguish between secondary data and secondary literature. The former (secondary data) are data from any source, including colleagues and professionals from other sectors. Secondary literature is information derived from more formal sources, such as journals, reports and papers, written mainly by academics, that we can use to support our own knowledge of our community work. These undoubtedly overlap, but we intend to discuss them separately in this chapter. Table 14.1 is an extract from an annual population survey that illustrates the previous case study and helped Kirsty to identify need.

The following case study shows how secondary data relating to crime rates illustrated the worth and value of a community football programme.

Joan is a community worker and knows through local knowledge that there is an issue of antisocial behaviour among young people in her town, so she started a football team to provide an alternative pursuit for young people. A year after the football club was launched, a local police officer told Joan that the crime rate among young people had gone down dramatically, something that the officer ascribed to the football team.

Secondary data is information from another source that triangulates your own observations. The police officer in the previous case study was able to verify information held by Joan on the value of the football club. We are aware that there is a danger of secondary data being deemed dull and dry, but it is crucial to showing the impact of what we do, and it can in fact be vivid and imaginative. We like to think of secondary data/literature as being on a continuum of formality, with anecdotal evidence at one extreme and statistics in formal academic literature at the other. Anecdotal evidence, on the one hand, may simply be a colleague's opinion of your project. On the other hand, formal data may include figures on crime rates, household surveys or census information; it may also be derived from the management information systems of other organisations.

Often our secondary data lie between these two poles and may include participation statistics from colleagues or progression from one project to another, such as progression by a migrant refugee from an initial course in English for Speakers of Other Languages (ESOL) to an employment course.

Table 14.1: Annual population survey

	Numerator	Per cent	Numerator	Denominator	Per cent	Confidence	Numerator	Denominator	Per cent	Confidence
Aged 16–64 employment rate – white	60,100	65.3	2,414,900	3,233,100	74.7	1.0	26,813,400	35,241,900	76.1	0.3
Aged 16–64 employment rate – ethnic minority	2,700	61.1	103,000	175,400	58.7	5.8	3,754,700	5,843,800	64.3	1.1
Aged 16–64 employment rate – white males	27,600	62.4	1,225,600	1,580,600	77.5	1.3	14,102,700	17,597,200	80.1	0.5
Aged 16–64 employment rate – ethnic minority males	1,700	69.5	60,800	84,500	72.0	7.6	2,055,100	2,820,700	72.9	1.4
Aged 16–64 employment rate – white females	32,500	68.0	1,189,300	1,652,500	72.0	1.3	12,710,800	17,644,700	72.0	0.5
Aged 16–64 employment rate – ethnic minority females	1,000	50.7	42,200	90,900	46.4	8.2	1,699,700	3,023,100	56.2	1.5

(continued)

Table 14.1: Annual population survey (continued)

	Numerator	Per cent	Numerator	Denominator	Per cent	Confidence	Numerator	Denominator	Per cent	Confidence
Percentage of population aged 16+ who are of mixed ethnic group	700	0.6	17,700	4,407,100	0.4	0.1	566,700	52,685,400	1.1	0.1
Percentage of population aged 16+ who are Indian	!	!	22,700	4,407,100	0.5	0.1	1,286,100	52,685,400	2.4	0.1
Percentage of population aged 16+ who are Pakistani/Bangladeshi	1,300	1.1	43,600	4,407,100	1.0	0.2	1,262,200	52,685,400	2.4	0.1
Percentage of population aged 16+ who are Black or Black British	700	0.6	30,800	4,407,100	0.7	0.1	1,468,300	52,685,400	2.8	0.1
Percentage of population aged 16+ who are of other ethnic group	2,000	1.7	65,900	4,407,100	1.5	0.2	1,745,800	52,685,400	3.3	0.1

(continued)

Table 14.1: Annual population survey (continued)

	Numerator	Per cent	Numerator	Denominator	Per cent	Confidence	Numerator	Denominator	Per cent	Confidence
Percentage of population aged 16–64 who are of mixed ethnic group	700	0.7	17,700	3,412,200	0.5	0.2	546,000	41,114,100	1.3	0.1
Percentage of population aged 16–64 who are Indian	!	!	21,700	3,412,200	0.6	0.2	1,132,200	41,114,100	2.8	0.1
Percentage of population aged 16–64 who are Pakistani/ Bangladeshi	1,000	1.1	42,700	3,412,200	1.3	0.2	1,187,400	41,114,100	2.9	0.1
Percentage of population aged 16–64 who are Black or Black British	~	0.5	30,100	3,412,200	0.9	0.2	1,353,000	41,114,100	3.3	0.1
Percentage of population aged 16–64 who are of other ethnic group	2,000	2.0	63,300	3,412,200	1.9	0.3	1,625,200	41,114,100	4.0	0.1

Source: ONS (simplified and derived from Nomis on 19 March 2018)

Figure 14.1: Example of secondary data

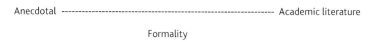

Anecdotal --- Academic literature

Formality

From Figure 14.1, we can see that secondary data may be anecdotal. Take the example of Martina, a health worker, at one end of the continuum. One of her colleagues told Martina that he had heard that a programme of yoga classes for users of alcohol and drugs was instrumental in users' progression to abstinence, because of the relaxation induced by the yoga. As the organiser of the yoga classes, Martina was particularly pleased.

At the other end of the continuum, academic literature could be used in this case to illustrate the relationships between stress and use of alcohol and drugs in the general adult population. Both ends of the continuum will be useful to Martina, and there are many things that lie between anecdote and academic literature on the continuum, such as media reports, feedback from participants and health statistics.

Secondary data: using information and data to inform community practice

This following case study focuses on change taking place as a result of access to data through partner channels.

Background

A spike in vandalism in Town A was emerging. Initial police response identified a developing gang culture among 15 to 18-year-olds. This coincided with the increased vandalism, along with a rise in numbers of local accident and emergency cases in this age group. Concern was rising among professionals in related areas of work in the community. The issue had taken them by surprise.

Partners in Town A met periodically to discuss developments and collaborative working in relation to local issues. Membership of this group included police officers, local authority youth work staff, health professionals, secondary school guidance staff and others. Following discussion with community youth work staff, a meeting was called at short notice to look at the emerging picture. A key function of this meeting was to look at the facts, scrutinise existing data and adjust services if necessary. This group was new to sharing data – working relationships were good, but collective approaches had not yet included access to a full range of partner information.

The turning point in this partner meeting was scrutiny of data over a period of 12 months across a number of agency data management information systems. This showed that there had indeed been a build-up of tension and related youth crime, which was appearing on the horizons of all professional groupings involved, but in isolation had not registered wider concern. The local community centre was temporarily closed for building works, bus services between towns had been reduced, and the number of young people in the age bracket concerned was unusually high. Sudden unemployment was affecting families in a number of different ways.

However, the resources and activities of partner bodies were not being adjusted to take account of the issues. Services had been delivered routinely based on historical practice rather than need. All partners had access to their own internal management information systems, but the scrutiny of data was passive rather than active. Trends captured in separate data management systems, when looked at as a whole, showed the danger spots and thus the potential for relevant action.

Activity

Immediate engagement with the young people involved was established. Youth work staff were crucial in identifying the key issues with the help of the young people, and resources based on historical deployment were adjusted as new priorities emerged.

A peer-led approach, supported by community youth work staff, worked in the geographical area, and learning and development activities were planned in conjunction with relevant partners. Partners provided the funding for a short-term outreach centre while long-term action was identified.

Outcomes and impact

- Services were more accurately targeted to address issues relating to young people in the locality.
- Reduced levels of youth vandalism and of health and safety danger were apparent.
- Improved and purposeful communication between partners and increased confidence in using shared data was manifest.

Key messages

- Needs-led services are dependent on an accurate picture that can be provided by available data and intelligence.
- Partner data can be crucial in determining an accurate picture in planning and delivering community learning and development (CLD) activity. We cannot know it all ourselves as CLD practitioners and services, although being holders of local knowledge is usually a strength in CLD practice. Locally gathered data, combined with local knowledge and national indicators of need, are essential in targeting scarce resources.

At times, we need to take stock and adjust services and resources, but to do this confidently we need to know what is needed.

Management information systems can give us important data, although we must, of course, be alert to analysis of what these data tell us.

Secondary data are often linked to management information systems, discussed in Chapter 13. In our work as practitioners, we derive our own information from such a system, but we may also derive other information from the system to assist with calibration, analysis and triangulation of our own data. For example, we may derive data from an MIS on the numbers of people who have participated in our employment programme over the course of a year, and compare these data to the number of local people registered as unemployed. This allows us to calibrate the penetration of the employment programme by analysing the demography (age, gender identity, and so on) of those attending compared with those registered as unemployed, in order to show the impact of the programme.

Secondary data may be used at all stages of a project from inception to reporting, but perhaps are most commonly used in needs analysis and evaluation. For needs analysis, local statistical data can be very important. Changes in poverty status will have an impact on the health and wellbeing of many of our participants, and economic changes will have a similar impact for good or ill. Small changes like the closure of local shops will affect elderly people, whereas wider changes, such as a downturn in the economy, will affect those of working age.

Evaluation is an important point at which to use secondary data, as it helps us to illustrate the problem or issue on which we are working, and to demonstrate the importance and significance of the issue or service. It also helps us to triangulate by showing that others agree with our findings, whether our programme is effective, needs to be amended or has reached a natural conclusion.

The following case study illustrates the breadth of reasons for using secondary data and the range of information that can be used. It describes a project undertaken by Kirsty and colleagues to develop an ESOL Partnership Review and Development Plan for Dundee City Council.

The review was undertaken:

- to better understand the needs of ESOL learners;
- to review ESOL provision in the light of local and national guidance and changes in funding arrangements;
- to develop a better understanding of the roles of each of the partners in supporting the development of language skills, community involvement and cultural awareness;
- reduce duplication across providers;
- raise awareness of opportunities and identity resources;
- strengthen integrated ways of working across the partnership and identify pathways and progression routes or ESOL learners.

(Derived from Dundee City Council, 2018)

This case study shows the range of uses that can be supported by secondary data. The data used in the review consisted, among other things, of a population breakdown of the town; data on English proficiency; data from schools concerning English proficiency; and data showing where migrants settle. This was linked to data from Kirsty's own work (primary data) on, among other things, age, gender split, employment status, and why learners attended classes. Through this combination of primary and secondary data, the review resulted in a partnership ESOL vision statement and delivery priorities, and subsequent publication, demonstrating the effectiveness of the partnership and of the review undertaken by the partners.

Quality, relevance and usefulness

It is absolutely crucial before using secondary data to be critical of the data's quality, relevance and usefulness. This involves professional judgement to assess a wide range of complex criteria. Having established the quality, relevance and usefulness of the data, it is important to be mindful of how you make use of it in the context of your local situation or community.

Quality, relevance and usefulness are closely linked to questions of validity in research. Validity in research is a much-contested area, but here we take it to mean the validity of the data according to their quality and usefulness to us. So, with qualitative data, we suggest the need to use criteria such as authenticity, honesty and truthfulness to determine quality. Authenticity means that the data actually do what they say they will do and that interpretation of the data is, for example, not too far-fetched. Authenticity means that what the author or speaker has said about the information or data rings true. If a report states that obesity among young people is linked to gaming online but the writer has not asked the young people about snacking while playing, you may question the authenticity of the secondary data.

Honesty means that the secondary data have been interpreted honestly and not too much is made of a simple situation, for example. Truthfulness is a criterion that you can only judge by your feelings about the data. Do they feel right? Take the example of a study about a community that states that community spirit has increased, but does not address how this has been measured or noticed beyond citing the use of a community noticeboard. This is a bit too far-fetched to be real. You may be surprised by an outcome of a report and it may still feel right. For example, one of us, Karen McArdle, conducted a study of rural poverty with adults in Scotland and found that quality of housing in the cold weather mattered. She did the same study with young people in the same area and found it was of very little concern, which she thought was surprising. Moreover, if a report about a project cites only positive outcomes, we are usually right to be a bit suspicious. Work in the community is complex and never all good to the same extent; there are always areas for improvement. This does not mean, however, that the project in question is a 'bad' one. If secondary data feel wrong or limited, we are often tempted not to use them, but beware that if your reports are too unremittingly positive, they will lack credibility.

Relevance means that the data are transferable to your community from the context in which they were gathered. We avoid using the term generalisable here, as that has a particular meaning for quantitative data. Transferable for our purposes means that common sense tells you that a particular situation may well be applicable in your community. For example, if data show that a community next door to yours has set up a well-frequented food bank to alleviate poverty, you may find this helpful for securing funding for your own community for a similar project, as the levels of poverty, albeit not the same, are similar across the two communities.

You are the only one who can judge the usefulness of data relating to your project. Usefulness means that the data tell you something about your community and your activities, and add to or enhance your understanding of the community or project, as the following case study shows.

> A project with Aboriginal women in Western Australia that sought to set up a cooperative to sell artefacts struggled because the women did not attend the shop at the side of the road on a tourist route during opening hours. It was only when the community worker discovered that the women, who led a traditional lifestyle, had an understanding of time that was different from the Western understanding (more seasonal, less a daily time, associated with place) that it became clear that the project would not work despite best intentions.

Finding data that support what you are doing or wish to do is exciting, as it illustrates the importance and significance of what we do in the community. Sharing data is also important. Criteria for judging the quality of quantitative data are similar to those outlined earlier, but here the issue of generalisability is important. Quantitative data use statistical samples to show whether findings for a specific population can be considered to be relevant to a wider population. Quantitative data usually state whether they are generalisable to other populations, but if not you will need to make judgements about the size and nature of the relevant sample and to what extent it reflects your community or participants. One of Karen's projects, for example, involved a study in a county with 350,000 residents, examining the importance to people of individual government services. A sample was taken of 100 residents, which was considered to be representative of the population as a whole, as the sample was itself representative of age, gender and ethnicity. A study such as this will likely be representative of the whole population. The study found that most people were concerned about the quality of the roads, and the findings were used by the transport department to secure more funding for road maintenance. As the study concerned a mainly rural county, it would probably not apply to you if you worked in a city environment, so you would need to make judgements about the nature of the community who made up the sample.

Overall, when assessing the relevance and usefulness of the secondary data in particular, it is important to consider the data you intend to use to supplement your own in terms of 'who, what, where, when and how'. Secondary data need not be identical in their purpose of process to yours, but you will need to make judgements about the strength of their relevance and in what ways they are relevant. The following section examines the 'who, what, where, when and how' questions in turn.

Who, what, where, when and how

Let us begin by asking who the data describe. How similar is the sample to your population of participants? What kind of people are described – are they male, female, old or young? Are some people missing (for example, migrants, a particular ethnic group, disabled people)? If the population is different in the secondary data in some ways, does this matter and if so, why? For example, data that concern graffiti art as a successful engagement activity for young people in a city environment may not be relevant in a rural outback community, where adults may find such street art more offensive than city dwellers who are more used to it. If there are differences, you may still choose to use the data, explaining how they concern different people but are still relevant.

The next question to explore is the 'what' of your secondary data. What was done to get the secondary data and does that still mean they are relevant? If the secondary data concern the health of elderly people living on a particular street, obtained through questionnaires, ask yourself about whether the sample included those with literacy, writing or reading difficulties. You might also ask yourself how much detail about their health people are prepared to divulge in a questionnaire.

Another important question is to ask where the data were collected. Are the people in the data sample from the same culture? This may include the same country, the same rural/ suburban/city environment or the same set of streets in a town. It may also include where the people were from who are included in the data sample. Were the data collected at a shopping mall frequented mainly by people with high incomes? If so, is it relevant to your interest in shopping habits and relative poverty?

Next is the question of 'when'. If your data concern young people, education and school, for example, the data will be different if collected first thing on a Monday or last thing on a Friday. Similarly, there may be cultural factors that influence the times when people are available to be interviewed in the street or at a hospital accident and emergency facility. Once again, it is necessary to make a judgement about the quality and relevance of the secondary data in terms of your own situation and community. Recency is another consideration. Some aspects of society change rapidly, and it is important to consider how recent the secondary data are. For example, ethnic mix and presence of asylum seekers in some communities makes data irrelevant unless relevant to the past three years.

The following example from Kirsty's work as a locality-based community worker with a youth club shows how secondary data can be used as the basis for choosing priorities in community work and understanding situations in more depth.

Our team was asked by the local academy to do some work, one to one, with a third-year pupil who was becoming disengaged from education. The pupil had been caught smoking and was a regular truant. The school wanted to know if we could support this young person's wider achievement As a local team, we received many such requests from the school but, as a relatively small team, we did not have the capacity to respond to every such request, nor should we. Youth work has three essential and definitive features, which are not always compatible with every referral we receive. These are:

- young people choose to participate;
- the work must build from where young people are;
- youth work recognises the young person and the youth worker as partners in a learning process (YouthLink Scotland, 2005).

Within a couple of weeks of this request, we were contacted by a community police officer, who was concerned about a number of antisocial complaints he had received about a couple of boys in one of the villages in which both he and I worked. Further discussion with our police colleague revealed that one of the boys was in the same situation as the young person, about whom we had been contacted by the school. The young people had yet to be charged with any offence, but the police officer was concerned that unless there was some intervention, that was how things were going to end up – with charges.

Having received a concern about this young person from the school, backed up with the police officer's statistical data and anecdotal evidence, we decided that we needed to engage with this group of young people in the village in which they lived. We decided to visit the village one evening to do some street work. We hoped to meet the young people in question to find out more information.

We were lucky, in that on the first evening we visited, we were able to very quickly meet up with the group and spend around an hour getting their perspective. Taking their feedback into consideration – that they were bored, as there was nothing to do in the village, and that they felt disrespected by community leaders – along with the information about their engagement with education and data from the police, we cautiously agreed to visit the village for six weeks to support the young people to identify their priorities for their community and for alternative activities.

This was very successful and led to the young people starting a youth group for any young person from the village, including those with whom they had previously had difficult relationships. We also accompanied some of these young people to address a meeting as part of a national review of strategic police priorities, ensuring

that they, as young people who had had involvement with the
criminal justice system, also had their voices heard.

This case study highlights that, as community workers, we
may trust some secondary data more than others. Here, the
information from the police was taken more seriously than the
request from the school. However, the community workers
did not commit to a youth programme in response to someone
else's data without carrying out their own initial engagement to
establish if there was, indeed, a need.

'How' is the final question to consider when reviewing
secondary data. How exactly were the data collected? Were they
collected by an external researcher or by the practitioner? It is
often assumed that an external researcher will be more objective
in any given situation, and it is similarly often believed, though
not said in so many words, that practitioners are more biased. It is
also thought that participants are less likely to be negative about
an experience with the facilitator than with an outside researcher.
One could simply dismiss these assumptions, but, when thinking
about how secondary data have been collected, it is important
to consider bias and to critique the research process to see how
it could have affected the secondary data and, therefore, their
relevance to our primary situation. As practitioners, we have
both seen evaluations comprising simple questionnaires that
require the participant to choose emoticons such as smiley faces
or other items denoting mood or facial expression. While these
have the advantage of speediness and obviate the need for high
levels of literacy among participants, they are of very little value
in community work.

It is important to remember that your situation is almost
always going to be different from the situation described in the
secondary data, but you can compare and contrast the primary
and secondary data in your presentation. It may be that the
secondary data have only tentative links to your situation, but
they may still be a very useful addition, because they make you
think in different ways about your own community. For example,
during work on why some rural communities are very close-knit
and closed to community work, Karen did some background

reading on culture. This triggered the ideas mentioned in Chapter 1 about former fishing communities facing outwards, away from other people and towards the sea, and becoming very self-reliant over the centuries, a situation compounded by the decline in Scotland of the fishing industry and residents' negative experience of economic interference from outside.

Being critical

The previous section describes how to be critical of secondary data in whatever form they appear. Being critical does not mean being negative, however. Hughes and colleagues (2010) describe critical skills as carefully judging the soundness of arguments and suggest that there are three dimensions to this:

- interpreting meanings in an argument;
- determining, as much as possible, the truth (or likely truth) of statements;
- assessing whether a premise links to a conclusion.

Interpreting meanings in an argument entails being conscious of what exactly is being said by the writer or speaker. In our context, as community workers, this means making links between what is argued and our own experience and knowledge. How would you decide, for example, what social capital means when used in the context of a report that considers it to be important to young people's career prospects? In our experience, we have found that competing definitions of social capital are used in relation to young people and are generally no more than parents' social capital. In being critical, we must understand exactly what is being said or claimed.

Determining the truth of statements, or probability of truth, is crucial to being critical. This involves making careful judgements, and although judgements are by definition subjective, they can be based on considered opinion. Such careful judgement can be broken down into the 'who, what, where, when and how' discussed above. Truth is a very moveable feast and is rarely black and white, but we can usually tell implicitly if something feels right. If it feels wrong or does not sit well with your experience, it is important to explore your own feelings and the source of the discomfort.

The third dimension involves assessing whether the basis or premise of the argument links to the conclusions made. A premise is an assumed proposition, for example, stating that a particular intervention/project has been effective. In order to be critical of this statement, we need to understand the project's purpose, the quality of evidence that suggests its effectiveness, and what has been achieved in relation to its purpose.

These three dimensions work together and we rarely think of these processes separately, but each is important to judging the quality of the secondary data we encounter.

Secondary literature

Secondary literature is a term used here to describe the reading you do to maintain your professional knowledge. It may also provide the secondary data you use to illustrate aspects of your work in the community. The literature underpins your professional knowledge and helps to keep you up to date with developments in the field, while the secondary data are used with a particular purpose in mind.

Secondary literature may include research or project reports, academic writings, books, reports in the media and blogs. The way to access this information is to be an engaged professional who maintains networks. Online networks frequently report on writing that is relevant to the practitioner. There are many search engines that can be used to search for literature against keywords, and the findings can usually be sourced at a local or university library. There are different power dynamics associated with the different types of literature. For example, academic literature, which must be peer-reviewed, is considered to be very strong and carries a certain *éclat*. By the same token, society, as evidenced by prevalence in the media, values quantitative data in the form of percentages and generalisability above other forms of data. You can use this to your advantage in terms of using secondary literature, but it is important to be aware that this is a social power dynamic and that the opinion of one expert and the opinion of one participant can be of equal importance.

Networks

Networks are one of the most important factors in accessing information, data and literature to support your professional knowledge. Networks may comprise online or face-to-face contact, even an informal chat over coffee. The most important aspect of networks is that they must be maintained by an infrequent chat or online blog or post, or perhaps a phone call to register and maintain interest.

We hope that you will choose to use secondary data as a matter of course. Even if it is time-consuming, it is too easy to dismiss it using this argument, especially when it is crucial not only to professional effectiveness but also to being seen to be effective. In our opinion, too much evidence gathering consists of doing a feedback questionnaire, planned and implemented at the conclusion of an activity without any reference to secondary data – in short, meaning that the primary data are not triangulated.

Presenting your primary and secondary data

Chapter 4 provides suggestions for how to present your primary and secondary data. Here we focus on the ethical dimensions of being critical of secondary data. It is quite possible to be very negative about others' work, but it is important to respect our own data and that of others. Moreover, it is possible to use the critical skills of 'practised arguing' to, in effect, lie about our data or the data of others. Hughes and colleagues (2010: 27) describe the moral dilemmas of being critical tellingly:

> Like any skill, critical thinking skills can be used for good or ill. There are many ways in which they can be abused. They can be used to make a bad argument look much stronger than it really is and to make an opponent's position look much weaker than it really is. They can be used to make ourselves look wise and others look foolish. They can be used to avoid having to respond to legitimate criticism and to persuade others to change their beliefs for inadequate reasons.

Respecting others, and being open-minded and constructive, are important dimensions of the judgements we make in criticality.

When presenting our findings, we are aiming to create an argument. The following questions may help us think about how we present our primary data and the secondary data that illuminates them.

- Is the problem or issue clearly defined and is its importance established?
- What is my personal perspective concerning the primary data and have I communicated this?
- Have I dealt with the secondary data/literature in a thorough and balanced way?
- How good was my method – who, what, where, when and how?
- Are my conclusions justified by a combination of the primary and secondary data?
- What are the strengths and limitations of all the data I have found (including my own)?
- Does my discussion hold together?
- Is my work written/spoken for the right audience?

It is important to consider how much secondary data or literature to use. Once again, this is a judgement for you to make, but your own data are the most important part of a presentation.

Challenge questions

1. What data do you hold about work in the community?
2. What data do you have that illuminate your work in the community?
3. How can you use these secondary data to link to your own data?
4. How can you use these two forms of data to demonstrate the impact of what you do?

References

Dundee City Council (2018) *Dundee ESOL Partnership Review and Development Plan: 2018–2020*, Dundee: Dundee City Council.

Hughes, W., Lavery, J. and Doran, K. (2010) *Critical Thinking: Introduction to Basic Skills* (6th edn), London, ON: Broadwater Press.

Youthlink (2005) *Statement on the Nature and Purpose of Youth Work*, available at https://www.youthlinkscotland.org/media/1255/statementonthenatureandpurposeofyouthwork.pdf (accessed 24 March 2020).

15

Knowing ourselves: self-evaluation

Sue Briggs and Karen McArdle

Introduction

Three key questions lie at the heart of self-evaluation. These are:

How are we doing?

- Are we providing appropriate, accessible high-quality services/ activities/opportunities?
- Are we setting and achieving ambitious targets?
- Are we systematically improving the quality of what we offer?

How do we know?

- Are we gathering evidence to assess how we are doing?
- Are we continuously measuring and evaluating the impact of the services/activities/opportunities we provide?

What are we going to do now?

- Are we using the evidence we have gathered to support our strong outcomes and change those that need more development?
- Are we using robust evidence to plan for future developments, so they best meet the needs of those we work with and other stakeholders?

(Education Scotland, 2016: 41)

Self-evaluation is founded on the principle that we want to characterise our work by the quality of what we do and that self-evaluation helps us to know whether this quality is, indeed, present. It is also important for keeping ourselves on track and avoiding getting lost in the paperwork of every day, at the expense of what we should be doing as our main professional purpose. It is a process of checking our quality and purpose, and leads to identifying outcomes for our community work so that we can then evaluate it.

In this chapter we focus on a systematic framework for self-evaluation that builds a baseline for reflection. This kind of framework may not exist where you work, but the principles still apply. A framework for self-evaluation provides a safety net that prevents us from falling into self-delusion. It allows us to stop and check what we do and ensure good, effective work. The backbone of effective self-evaluation is the morale of staff; it depends on morale and, indeed, increases morale. This morale increase is a product of the awareness of the community worker of what exactly is working and what can be done to improve practice. It is an affirmation of their practice.

A system of self-evaluation is very important for providing consistency and checks and balances about what is being done in professional practice, and a framework for self-evaluation in a team or across a profession can provide consistency of language and a common agreed purpose for the work. The process is important for accuracy of reporting and identifying where mistakes have been made or where change has occurred and practice needs to move on. The processes we use or are encouraged to use may be flawed or outdated, and it is important to pinpoint such problems in order to rectify them. A system of self-evaluation means that everyone in a team or across teams evaluates their own work in the same way. Nobody should be excluded; everyone can participate if it is part of the work–planning process. The findings of the self-evaluation system can be used to frame future work and development for staff. The system requires commitment from managers and a facilitative and supportive demeanour in terms of providing feedback and supporting staff to make changes to their practice.

The pros and cons of self-evaluation

The advantages of self-evaluation include the fact that it provides participants with detailed feedback and celebration of their experience and role in the development of the service or activities offered. For the practitioner, there is validation of practice and an opportunity to experience an enhanced quality of practice; self-evaluation boosts morale. It is a process that is intrinsic to planning for the future and can generate in an organisation an ethos of self-improvement, which leads to the ability to work to meet the goals of the profession. It also provides a confident and convincing picture of what we do in community work. Another advantage is that it develops a community worker's writing skills beyond narrative into evaluative judgement and we return to this later in this chapter.

One disadvantage of self-evaluation is that it can be risky; it poses a personal and professional risk, in that it may expose a lack of quality in what you do, and, if handled badly, may be confrontational. We consider, however that it is worth the risks for the validation it provides of work in the community, and this is good for our visibility with employers, funders and the general public. Another disadvantage is that successful self-evaluation takes time and commitment, but we would argue that it is well worth the effort and is, indeed, essential, if we are committed to knowing the value of what we do. We often hear community workers say they do not have time for this kind of paper-based activity, because there are other demands on their time, namely from participants. We argue that this is a short-sighted view, however, because self-evaluation is germane to the quality of the actual work done with participants.

Identity

> Cradle to grave, we perennially refer to our selves to make sense of our conduct and experience, and to guide related actions. The self in other words, is not only something we are, but an object we actively construct and live by. (Holstein and Gubrium, 2000: 10)

This quotation refers to the idea that we actively construct who we are and how we behave. This is central to self-evaluation, whereby we focus on self and what we do in our professional practice. Individual identity is the basis for many of the decisions and choices we make about our lives. It is in part a social experience in that we understand ourselves according to the reactions of others to who we are and what we do. We may have many social selves in that there are different aspects to our lives, where we meet different kinds of people. Individuals are active in the social world influenced by culture and society to behave in certain ways but also, they influence this themselves, in a feedback loop. Riessman (2008) describes in a metaphor the inner gyroscope, which balances the wide circle of other people one meets in one's life, or the competing voices of competing authorities. Being aware of this gyroscope and its use is an important dimension of professional practice where competing demands frequently arise and must be balanced using a certain maturity. This is something we can do for ourselves to manage the feelings arising from self-evaluation, or help others do the same.

Self-evaluation is underpinned by moral judgements and it is important to be aware of these. In aiming to undertake 'good' or 'effective' work in the community, we make judgements about exactly what is good for that community. This needs to be linked to the notion of the social self, where feedback from peers or participants governs what we do, so that we are not acting as the all-knowing professional but are representing expressed and considered requirements in a community setting.

Judgement

Judgement is a key component of evaluation, including self-evaluation. We place value on ideas. We should be cognisant of the values that underpin our judgements. Social values develop, merge and change over time, so it is critical that we analyse and consider the values that underpin what we do – our own values and those of the people for whom we work or volunteer. The following quotation suggests that the values that underpin communities influence the possibilities that are open to them, including opportunities, prohibitions and behavioural requirements.

> Moral codes, whether religious or secular, grow out of social structures and needs. As communities evolve, so do the duties and obligations of their members to each other, and the possibilities, social and moral, that are open to them. (Malik, 2014: 58)

We propose that all professional moral codes possess two elements: a set of values to pursue and a reason for pursuing those values (Malik, 2014). To put it another way, they express the means of doing good and show the end to which the values take us. Values may be explicit – for example, valuing inclusion and diversity in the context of a profession – or implicit, for example, valuing relationships as an individual. When we assess quality, for instance, we assess the dimensions of a project that we think contribute to the concept of 'quality'. Your idea of quality may be different from ours, so it is important to understand what is meant by quality. This is based on the value of what you believe is 'good' for an individual or community. Politicians are often very good at 'knowing' what is good for a population or community; we need to know our own opinion on this matter and be prepared to justify, adapt and challenge it when evidence suggests we are wrong.

Process

A process or framework for self-evaluation is important. Because it is linked to planning, self-evaluation is usually an annual event, enabling us to capture evidence at an early stage of a project or service cycle. The process of taking stock and engaging in a review cycle requires commitment from managers and staff alike. Managers must ensure that all staff are involved in the process, and all should be willing to engage in peer review. An underpinning principle of self-evaluation is honesty, founded on feedback from peers and participants. If this is not present in your organisation, you should seek to introduce it. The following sections suggest ways of managing the process for yourself.

Challenging ourselves

Challenge questions are a stimulus for reflection and for considering the quality of professional practice. Here, we select challenge questions aimed at improving overall performance and measuring the extent to which our work meets the needs of our participants and its level of impact on the local community. These are derived from Education Scotland's (2016) evaluation resource, *How Good is the Learning and Development in our Community?*, and could be adapted to any community work practice. They may be used in planning and evaluative cycles as part of supervision and peer review of projects, services and performance, and are intended to be challenging and to require reflection on the part of those engaged in professional practice.

Improvements in performance

- How well are our priorities and plans informed by high-quality analysis of current statistical and other information?
- How well informed is our analysis of needs? How well do we meet needs identified through strategic analysis?
- What evidence do we have of positive impacts and wider benefits resulting from partners' work?
- Does analysis and reporting of data demonstrate improvement? Are trends in performance improving over time?
- How well do we share information across partnerships and wider stakeholders?
- How well does our benchmarking and use of comparative information demonstrate improvement? Do we set challenging targets that lead to improvement?
- How well do our systems demonstrate progress against outcomes and targets? Does shared analysis of data among partners demonstrate effective performance in achieving intended outcomes?

Impact on participants

- How well do we meet the needs of participants? What evidence do we have that we are making a positive and sustained impact on their lives?
- How do we know that we are targeting the 'seldom heard' individuals/families in the community?
- What evidence do we have that learners are achieving, attaining and progressing?
- How well do we reflect the context of learners' lives, address barriers and meet their individual and community needs? How do we record this and address any concerns raised by participants?
- How do we ensure that learners are actively engaged in shaping their own learning?
- How well do we ensure that learners are involved in service design and improvement?
- How do we work with others to support learners to acquire skills for learning, life and work?
- How clear are participants' pathways?
- How well do we use accredited learning opportunities to raise and encourage participants to progress? How well do we value, support and actively promote fairness, equity and diversity?

Impact on the local community

- How well do we support communities to be strong resilient, supportive, influential and inclusive? What difference does this make?
- What evidence do we have that the individuals, groups and communities we work with are more confident, skilled, active and influential as a result of our input?
- How well do we develop relationships and partnerships with communities? How well do we support communities to improve and increase networking? How effective are these partnerships and networks?
- How well do we support individuals, groups and communities to increase their connection to place?

- How well do we support community groups and organisations to plan, manage and evaluate their work?
- How well are communities encouraged to be inclusive and value social and cultural diversity?
- How effectively do we support the communities we work with? How do we measure this?

The Education Scotland (2016) resource includes evidence that links to the challenge questions and illustrations and examples of 'very good' practice.

Peer review

Peer review is a strong and challenging process that may be founded on feedback from participants. It requires strong and sound mediation to ensure that its purpose remains positive. The process may be part of team supervision or may be managed between separate teams with a similar function. Peer review draws on the shared and combined expertise within and/or between professions. It is a process of social reflection. Social reflection is a term used to describe involving others in a vigorous, active capacity in an individual's process of reflection, rather than involving them as just an affirming listener (McArdle, 2018)

Evaluative writing

As discussed earlier, self-evaluation aims to establish the strengths of a given activity and to identify any actions that will bring about improvement. Self-evaluation draws on the widest possible range of evaluative materials as evidence, in order to determine the quality of a piece of work from a variety of perspectives. Capturing a picture to support this process depends on the quality of thinking and writing.

Writing demands a particular way of thinking that is very useful in self-evaluation. It demands an ability to synthesise, categorise and make sense of ideas, and then to express them in an understandable way. Here, we focus on evaluative writing in particular, which aims to improve the ways in which we think about, share and report on the success of our self-evaluation.

The following list provides other suggested reasons for focusing on evaluative writing.

- to assist with improvement of a service/project;
- to capture an accurate picture of how you are doing;
- to assist development of new/existing services;
- to record strengths of a project;
- to record weaknesses of a project;
- to promote reflection and debate;
- to provide a basis for planning;
- to demonstrate accountability;
- to report on quality and standards;
- to report on performance;
- to improve decision making;
- to encourage action;
- to reassure staff and participants;
- to help manage change.

The purpose of this section is to help you differentiate between descriptive, analytical, evaluative and reflective writing, which may be used for different purposes in an evaluative process. Descriptive writing is not helpful for self-evaluation in itself, but contributes to scene setting. Analytical writing looks for categories, patterns and trends in what you have found out. Evaluative writing considers what you mean by what you have found out, what your evidence tells you, and what your judgement is about that evidence. Reflective writing is your considered opinion about the experience, and focuses quite deliberately on the future and the change or action that will, or should, result from your evidence.

Evaluative statements are judgements that may be made in the following terms in an evaluation:

- judgements in terms of national priorities;
- judgements in terms of authority/local government/agency priorities;
- judgements in terms of team priorities;
- judgements in terms of previous best standard or performance;
- judgements in terms of improvement;

Box 15.1 Features of four types of writing used in self-evaluation

Descriptive writing

• Provides introductory and background/contextual information
• Lists, catalogues and outlines the way things are
• Does not establish relationships between ideas

Analytical writing

• Explores relationships of ideas or parts of something
• Provides possible situations and alternative responses
• Compares and contrasts

Evaluative writing

• Involves making a judgement about the quality of something
• Outlines implications and solutions, draws conclusions and makes recommendations
• Views something from many different angles, or questions something in order to ascribe value

Reflective writing

• Uses a reflection or review model to document experience or learning that takes place, and future steps/actions.

(Derived from Briggs, 2015: 4)

• judgements in terms of 'accepted' good practice;
• judgements illustrated through description;
• judgements in terms of agreed scales (that have agreed criteria of value)
• judgements in terms of agreed ratings or criteria;
• professional judgements;
• judgements in terms of outcomes;

- judgements in terms of expectations;
- judgements in terms of amount;
- judgements in terms of comparison.

For example, you might link your project to national priorities set by the government to show how these government priorities are being met, or you might show how your work is contributing to effective and accepted good practice as determined by your profession.

It is important that your evaluative statements are underpinned by evidence so that they are not just assertions or your unconsidered opinion. You cannot use such statements unless you have the evidence to back them up. It is hoped that this book will have helped with ways of collecting evidence. It is usual to keep evidence, as people may want to see it. Emotive language is usually out of place in evaluative statements. Positive statements must be accurate at the same time.

Self-evaluation leading to improved community service delivery

The following case study focuses on the role self-evaluation played in developing services run by local volunteers and the support of community practitioners in this process.

Background

Local community volunteers were involved in running a valued community project in Town B. This project focused on developing services and activities for older residents and had been running for five years. It had been established with local funding to address issues of isolation and to improve access to services relating to health and wellbeing.

Funding was coming to an end. Lobbying for additional funds was hampered by the lack of clarity by project leaders on what was now needed and what value it would bring.

Activity

Local community staff supported the group of volunteers to undertake a 'stock take' exercise reflecting on the work of the project over the five years, to focus on what was successful and what worked less well and to arrive at an informed view of what was now needed. This was designed as a formal self-evaluation exercise, the quality of which was dependent on the evidence gathered by project staff and volunteers and underpinning areas for development going forward.

Key to the evidence gathered was feedback from participants themselves on what had changed for them in their lives, from partner agencies in the form of statistical data, and from the volunteers who recognised the benefits to themselves and their community. Those involved became more confident in the case they were preparing for funders, as they understood the impact and outcomes of their project activity.

They also valued the role of experienced community staff in providing support for an exercise that encapsulated what was needed through effective reflection, a coherent picture captured and future planning to meet the needs in their community.

Outcomes/outputs

- Boost to the morale of volunteers and project participants when a comprehensive picture of what had been achieved was presented.
- Success in additional funding through an accurate depiction of what had been achieved.
- Confident plan for next steps delivery in this project.

Key messages

It is important to know how we are doing. We cannot successfully adjust and improve unless we take stock periodically. This applies to ourselves, as practitioners, as a quality management aspect of our work, but also when we work with others. This is important for the following reasons:

- feedback identifying outcomes and impact from everyone involved is crucial if we want to show effectiveness and success;
- our chances of retaining or increasing resources are increased when we have an accurate and confident picture of what has worked at hand. Effective future planning is underpinned by high-quality self-evaluation.

A final few words about self-evaluation: it is important to know yourself and to be open to feedback about your professional practice. It is, as we said at the beginning of this chapter, a little risky, but in order to improve, to change and to be better at what you do, self-evaluation is an important opportunity for learning.

Challenge questions

1. What self-evaluative processes do you engage in? How do you feel about self-evaluation?
2. What self-evaluative processes exist in your department or workplace?
3. When did you last receive peer feedback? How did you take it?

References

Briggs, S. (2015) *Evaluative Writing Handbook*, Aberdeen: Aberdeenshire Council.

Education Scotland (2016) *How Good is the Learning and Development in our Community?: Evaluation Resource*, Livingston: Education Scotland.

Holstein J.F. and Gubrium, J.F. (2000) *The Self we Live By: Narrative Identity in a Postmodern World*, Oxford: Oxford University Press.

Malik, K. (2014) *The Quest for a Moral Compass: A Global History of Ethics*, London: Atlantic Books.

McArdle, K. (2018) *Freedom Research in Education: Becoming an Autonomous Researcher*, Cham: Palgrave Macmillan.

Riessman, C.K. (2008) *Narrative Methods for the Human Sciences*, London: Sage.

PART III

Conclusion

16

Reflections: valuing community work

Sue Briggs, Kirsty Forrester, Ed Garrett, Karen McArdle and Catherine McKay

We have sought in this book to introduce approaches and methods practitioners can use to show the impact of what they do. The book has focused on community workers, but the greatest challenge we face as practitioners lies in recognition of the profession in which we work, which concerns us collectively, not individually. Increasingly in times of austerity, it is the developmental work embracing community work that is easy to cut in the short term, as it often has a longitudinal impact rather than meeting goals in political timescales of a short number of years. Working to show the effectiveness of individual projects does contribute to the overall esteem in which the profession is held, but we should also consider how we can foster esteem in other ways. A starting point is to consider the change we wish to make in the way which the profession is valued. We consider that this change lies in convincing people of the values that underpin what we do and the value of the principles that govern the ways that we work.

Working towards the wellbeing of the individual and community are at the core of our work and this brings together community workers from all disciplines. This provides a basis for cross-sectoral strength. The principles that underpin our work are also shared and provide a platform for cooperation across professions. The problem, if we accept that there is a problem, is that the approach is not well understood and we ourselves seem to find it difficult to communicate exactly what we do. This is because of the multifaceted and multilayered complexity discussed in Part I of this book. We need to be able to communicate the value and impact of our profession. The value, we suggest, lies in:

- working with individuals, groups and whole communities;
- working on issues identified, interpreted and managed at local level;
- working at the local level on issues with national and global significance;
- working sustainably with both a short-term and a longitudinal effect;
- working with people at all levels of society;
- sustaining useful and worthwhile relationships with all those involved in our work in order to effect change that is in the interests of the target community and wider society.

Much of this book has been about ethics and we should be aware that every choice we make in gathering evidence is political, and necessarily so. Complex questions of power, fake news and the nature of truth are germane to what we do as community workers and it remains for us to be aware of our own values and the value of what we do, and to stand up for this in the face of criticism, lack of knowledge and misunderstanding. This requires courage.

The work we do is important and sometimes it can appear that we are 'tinkering at the edges' of substantial problems. Poverty often underpins our work, and this is an intractable problem linked to economic and welfare systems in our own countries and in those on which we depend for trade and wellbeing. We cannot individually solve these problems, but coming together in collaboration makes our voices louder and harder to ignore. Many of us work in the community and value its importance, but we do not always look to cross-sectoral boundaries for support and influence. Where this happens, some very good work is possible. In the UK, the linking of health and social care disciplines has led to better joined-up working and greater influence for the social care sector. Such linking up can be done in many ways, from attending community conferences and participating in networks that link to our profession, to extending networks outside our own discipline.

Showing the impact of what we do is important for our profession as well as being important to us as individuals. It is important to be unafraid of broadcasting evidence of good practice, so that it can contribute to policy for community work and professional esteem. If we all do this as practitioners, we can contribute significantly to the esteem in which our profession is held − a profession that deserves esteem. Community work is a major contributor to social change. Looking at your government's policies, we would be surprised if they do not link to economic, employment, environment welfare, educational, health and planning reform, all of which have a community element. The power of community workers to assist with social change is undervalued by the profession itself and by policy makers. We must remedy this by gathering and showing evidence of the effectiveness of work in the community, and using this evidence both at the important local level and more broadly to influence wider decision making, thereby helping to solve seemingly intractable social problems.

Index

Page numbers in *italic* refer to figures in the text and in **bold** to tables.

Printed in Great Britain
by Amazon